MAMA BEAR

Apologetics®

**GUIDE TO
SEXUALITY DISCIPLESHIP
WORKBOOK**

HILLARY MORGAN FERRER
WITH TEASI CANNON

HARVEST HOUSE PUBLISHERS
EUGENE, OREGON

Published in association with the literary agency of Mark Sweeney & Associates.

For bulk, special sales, or ministry purchases, please call 1-800-547-8979.
Email: Customerservice@hhpbooks.com

Cover design and illustration by Amanda Hudson, Faceout Studio

Interior designed by Rockwell Davis

Mama Bear Apologetics® Guide to Sexuality Discipleship Workbook
Copyright © 2022 by Hillary Morgan Ferrer
Published by Harvest House Publishers
Eugene, Oregon 97408
www.harvesthousepublishers.com

ISBN 978-0-7369-8600-7 (pbk)
ISBN 978-0-7369-8601-4 (eBook)

CONTENTS

Part Three: Things That Are Tripping Everyone Up

WELCOME, AND HOW TO USE THIS STUDY GUIDE

Welcome! We at Mama Bear Apologetics are so excited to introduce you to the first-ever study *and* discipleship guide. Our sincere desire is that as you work through it, you will be gently challenged but not at all overwhelmed.

WHAT THE HECK IS A DISCIPLESHIP GUIDE?

We love our study guides. They help us better sift through the material and digest it so we can integrate it into our everyday lives. And in *Mama Bear Apologetics Guide to Sexuality*, we give a lot of practical tips for how to address these ideas with your kids. But what if we could have even *more* practical tips? More is better, right? (Unless you have something like scabies, and then less is generally better.)

As you read through this guide, you'll notice this icon: 🐾, which symbolizes a *discipleship opportunity*. With each discipleship opportunity comes an activity or conversation that will translate abstract ideas into a more concrete form so that little minds can better understand the concepts. We don't have specific ages attached to each opportunity, though we sometimes specify if the activity is for your older cubs.

Something we want everyone to keep in mind: The questions at the end of each chapter in your main book and the questions in this discipleship guide are all applicable for dinnertime discussions! Don't think that since you are going through these questions as an adult (or in a group of adults) that they can't be used for kids. Children from middle school on up should be able to track with the ideas presented here. So if at some point you want to grab another study guide and go through the process again with your middle schooler or high schooler, you can. And we encourage you to do so! It doesn't have to be labeled "teen guide" to still be applicable for teens.

Challenges to identity—both through gender and sexuality— are confusing, and we cannot underestimate the impact they are having on our children. It's time to take back some ground, Mama Bears! And as we do so, remember: We don't stand before God accountable for our successes. We stand before Him accountable for our *faithfulness*. So let's be faithful in stewarding these precious boys and girls under our care.

With that in mind, we want to share some tips on how to make the most of your reading and this guide.

Before you read a chapter in *Mama Bear Apologetics Guide to Sexuality*:

- We would love for you to have a four-color retractable click pen (flashback to high school!) on hand, but if you don't, grab four different colored pencils, pens, or highlighters and use a system similar to the one we recommend below.

- Have a dictionary or dictionary app ready for reference.

- Skim through the chapter's title and bold-print subheads to get an idea of what you're going to read. (This pre-reading strategy helps you get excited to dig in.)

- Think of a question or two you hope will be answered in the chapter.

- Pray and ask the Holy Spirit to guide you into all truth.

Lord God, our world is so broken. There is so much sexual confusion everywhere. Who am I? What can one person do? Open my eyes like the servant of Elisha, Lord. Let me see Your angels who are with me in the battle. I pray that You would remove any fear I have regarding this topic and plant my feet firm in Your truth. I pray that as You shepherd me into a biblical understanding of sex, that I would understand Your commandments for sex. And as I understand Your commandments, Lord, help me lead my children to understand the beauty of Your magnificent design.

While you read the chapter:

I have used this multicolor note-taking system for almost a decade. It has helped me to actively read and organize material so that, even years later, I can go back and glance through a book for its main points and my favorite quotes. The strategy suggested here is a simplified version of my system, so you can tweak it to what works best for you. I find that color-coding is helpful for future reference purposes:

- Black ink—draw a box around unfamiliar words and draw a squiggly line under the definition *if* it appears within the text. (Squiggly lines will help you distinguish definitions from general notes.) If the word is not defined, record definitions in the margins or at the back of the book. We recommend looking up the definitions right away!

- Blue ink—underline helpful passages for easy skimming. This will help you when you search through the book later for the main ideas.

- Green ink—use this color for content you have questions about. (I also draw a question mark in the margin.)

- Red ink or highlight—save this for the true "Aha!" moments or ideas you want to remember. (This is especially helpful for finding key quotes and thoughts in the future.)

After you read the chapter:

- Quickly skim through the chapter to review all the words you've underlined, highlighted, and written in the margins. (Look at all those colors. This is your pat on the back for being an active reader!)

- Jump into the study guide material for that chapter.

In each chapter of the study guide you will find an introductory thought followed by seven major sections. We want you to set your own pace, so we haven't divided the lessons or sections into specific days, but you could choose to work through one section a day. Here are the types of sections:

Active Reading Notes: Here you will record a few pre-, mid-, and post-reading thoughts, including vocabulary. Here's an example.

READING FOCUS	MY RESPONSE
Before You Read:	
After skimming the chapter title and subheads, what is one question you would like to have answered in the chapter?	*My question:* Why does sex matter?
While You Read:	
Vocabulary List three words you found in the chapter, and we will add a few more words we hope you will find and look up in the dictionary.	*My words:* Here, write down words that are unfamiliar to you, and make your best attempt to briefly record the definitions. *Book words:* Here, you'll find words that are defined in the book. Page numbers are given so that you can fill in the definitions in this space.

After You Read:	
Answer Did you find an answer to your pre-reading question? (We hope so.) If yes, write it down.	*My answer:* Sex matters because it helps us see and know God accurately.
"Aha!" moments List three things you highlighted or underlined in the chapter. This can be new information you learned, encouraging reinforcements of things you already knew, or just plain anything that popped out at you.	*My "Aha!" moments:* 1. 2. 3.

Pick a Question: As you're using this study guide, it's easy to forget that there are already study questions in the main book. Use this space as an opportunity to review the questions and respond to the one you find most thought-provoking.

Empowering Words: Supplemental and significant vocabulary will be given here.

Empowering Thoughts: Supplemental or reinforcing thoughts will be included here.

Digging Deeper: Here we will ask some guiding questions to help you process what you've learned and further equip you to "ROAR Like a Mother." Be aware that not all questions are asking you to simply regurgitate what the book said. Many are intended to make you *think* through the material, draw connections, and wrestle through real-life scenarios. But don't worry! If you get stuck on a question, just move on until you feel more comfortable digging in. Or better yet, grab some girlfriends for coffee and discuss it! Whether or not you answer every single question, you *will* come away from this study guide with a much stronger grasp of what you're learning.

Key Scriptures: Here we've offered a few related verses that can help you reflect on what God says regarding the ideas presented in each chapter. We recommend journaling through each of them, evaluating *how* the passages reinforce or address the biblical perspective of the topic at hand.

PAWS for Prayer: Here you will be guided in a sweet time of prayer—a moment to take what you're learning to God and intentionally involve the Holy Spirit in your journey. The PAWS section has four steps:

- **PRAISE**—Identify the *attributes* of God that you have seen manifested lately. You may be thankful *for* a recent bonus, but you will want to *praise* God for being Jehovah Rapha, the God who provides. Or maybe you didn't get the bonus and you don't know why. *Praise* God for His omniscience and how He knows what you need when you need it, even if you don't understand. Praising God for *who* He is rather than *what* He does will help you orient your heart toward Him, no matter what is going on in your life, good or bad. If you need a little help with this section, I recommend Googling "attributes of God" or "names of God."

- **ADMIT**—Acknowledge the areas where you have blown it. Maybe you didn't trust God, or you acted in anger with your kids or husband. Whatever your dirty laundry, bring it to God here. He already knows your heart and wants to be with you as you learn to navigate this thing called the Christian life.

- **WORSHIP through thanksgiving**—Here is where you can thank God for specific things He has *done*. When you remember that all good things come from Him, you realize you have much to be thankful for.

- **SUPPLICATION (or SUBMIT your requests)**—
  After you have praised God for who He is, admitted where you are struggling, and worshipped through thanksgiving, then present your requests to Him. Sometimes God doesn't give us what we ask for because we ask with wrong motives (James 4:3). Or sometimes what we want would thwart something that He—in His goodness and knowledge—is doing in our lives that couldn't be accomplished if He answered our specific wish. But He still wants us to ask, and we can know that however He chooses to answer, it is for our good.

• • •

And don't forget! The discipleship opportunities are not in their own section. Every time you see a 🐾, we have provided you with activities or conversations to have with your kids.

Part One

THINGS I PROBABLY ALREADY KNEW...BUT KINDA FORGOT

In part one, we learn how God defines sex and what He desires to communicate through human sexuality. We learn about the power of sex and how destructive it is when misused. We also define and explain the wonderful aspects of a biblical worldview, including how it affects the way we view sexuality. We see that an incorrect view of sex can lead to an incorrect view of God and His heart—including His good designs and His love for all humanity.

We hope the following pages will shed light on the cultural confusion you're likely experiencing related to all things sex. We also hope to empower you to have God-honoring convictions and conversations with your friends, neighbors, and children, and to find hope and peace in God's good design for His creation. Our goal is to equip you to share that hope with a hurting world in need of truth and love.

LESSON 1

SEXUALLY
SET
APART

G od's commands regarding sex are not just a side issue. They are a prominent theme spanning the Old and New Testaments, especially in terms of holiness. The word "holy" literally means "set apart for a special purpose." As Christians, our sexual ethic is a major way in which we are called to be set apart from the world because sexual holiness is, in essence, a *sign of our knowledge of and commitment to God.* It has always been this way.

Mama Bear Apologetics Guide to Sexuality, page 23

ACTIVE READING NOTES

READING FOCUS	MY RESPONSE
Before You Read:	
After skimming the chapter title and subheads, what is one question you would like to have answered in the chapter?	My question:
While You Read:	
Vocabulary List three words you found in the chapter in addition to the words we have provided.	My words: Book words: *postmodernism* (page 22)— *the argument from silence* (page 26)—
After You Read:	
Answer Did you find an answer to your pre-reading question? (We hope so.) If yes, write it down.	My answer:
"Aha!" moments List three things you highlighted or underlined in the chapter. This can be new information you learned, encouraging reinforcements of things you already knew, or just plain anything that popped out at you.	My "Aha!" moments: 1. 2. 3.

PICK A QUESTION

Use this space to review the study questions at the end of the chapter and respond to the one you find most thought-provoking or convicting.

EMPOWERING WORDS

- *Sufficiency of Scripture*—Scripture contains all the words that God intended His people to have at each stage of redemptive history, and it now contains what we need to know for salvation and trusting and obeying God perfectly (Deuteronomy 29:29).

- *Perspicuity (clarity) of Scripture*—According to this doctrine, you don't need a seminary degree to understand what God has said to you and what He wants for your life. The Bible's teachings can be understood by all who read it seeking God's help (Deuteronomy 6:6-7).

- *Sin*—Sin is any failure to conform to the moral law of God in act, attitude, or nature.

- *Sanctification*—This refers to the maturation of a Christian, progressively becoming more like Christ in heart, words, and action. Unlike the gift of salvation, the sanctifying process is hard work and involves our active and mindful participation.

EMPOWERING THOUGHTS

In this chapter we learn that "holiness" literally means "set apart for a special purpose." On page 33, we read that one of the defining characteristics of Christ's followers is sexual holiness. While sexual holiness is a significant defining characteristic of Christ-followers and reflects essential truths to those around us, we must remember it's not the primary purpose of the gospel or the ultimate goal of Christian life.

1. Read the following verses and record what they say about our primary goal as followers of Christ.

    Philippians 3:10-12:

    Hebrews 13:21:

 ## What Does It Mean to Be Set Apart?

What items do you have lying around your home or office that are set apart for special use? A LEGO set? A special dress? Video game controllers? What about things that have a particular use and would be ruined were you to misuse them? (Like contacts. You can't really use contacts for anything other than seeing. And if you do...well...you probably shouldn't put them back in your eyes!) Start creating this category in your child's mind so they have examples to draw from when you discuss that they as a Christian are to be holy—set apart for a special use.

DIGGING DEEPER

1. Read the paragraph that starts by describing the Asherah poles on page 25. What can we learn about the character and motives of the pagan gods from the type of worship they required? Compare your answers to the character and motives of Christ.

   Pagan gods

   Christ

2. In the first paragraph of the section called "The New Testament: Pointing Back to God's Design" on page 26, we are introduced to a common misinterpretation regarding Jesus' views on sexuality, especially homosexuality. It asserts that because Jesus doesn't explicitly condemn homosexuality, it must be condoned—at least in some measure. How is the argument from silence logically fallacious and theologically dangerous?

3. Read the verses listed on pages 27-28. How would you respond to a self-identified Christian who claims that Christians who reject other sexual expressions/orientations are misrepresenting God's heart, promoting harmful doctrines that hurt and

marginalize people whom God has called us to love? (Pay special attention to the Thessalonians passage.)

4. On page 30, we read, "What are you doing when you engage in the act of sex before committing to the covenant of marriage? Lying. You are lying. You are repeating a promise that you never made." Read the following verses, and record any thoughts you have regarding the potential ripple effects of this lie.

   1 Corinthians 6:18:

   Romans 1:24-32:

5. How might understanding sex as an act of "repeating marital vows in bodily form" change the way people view sex, even within a marriage? How might it change the way husbands approach or respond to their wives during intimate moments? What about wives to their husbands?

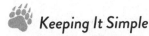 **Keeping It Simple**

This is where you can have some fun. Pick something random in your house—such as orange juice or a spatula—and then remind your kids constantly throughout the week everything it's *not* to be used for (washing the dog, waxing the car, cleaning up vomit...). Have them join in; I bet they'll get even more creative than you! When they've had about all they can take, ask them, "We had some fun with that, but do you think our extra instructions regarding [fill in the blank] were helpful? Stupid? Necessary? Unnecessary?"

Bring it back to God's Word and sexuality. The Bible doesn't claim to be an exhaustive book, detailing everything *not* to do. Instead, it provides us with a clear original design (Genesis 5:2), the original purpose (Genesis 1:28, 2:23-25), and maybe a *few* ways of misusing His good gift of sexuality (Leviticus 18 and 20). If your kids ever ask if an alternate sexuality or gender is a sin, simply respond with "What was God's original design?" Keep it simple.

KEY SCRIPTURES

We encourage you to read the following verses in context (meaning, read at least the entire chapter). Reflect on how they relate to what you're learning, and thank God for the hope and guidance found in His Word.

- 2 Timothy 2:21—"If anyone cleanses himself from what is dishonorable, he will be a vessel for honorable use, set apart as holy, useful to the master of the house, ready for every good work."

- Psalm 37:4—"Delight yourself in the LORD, and he will give you the desires of your heart."

- Romans 12:2—"Do not be conformed to this world, but be transformed by the renewal of your mind, that by testing you may discern what is the will of God, what is good and acceptable and perfect."

PAWS FOR PRAYER

In closing this chapter, reflect on what you learned in lesson 1 and journal your prayer to God here:

Praise:

Admit:

Worship with thanksgiving:

Supplication (ask):

SEX IS SPELLED W-O-R-L-D-V-I-E-W

Your children's grip on Christianity will only be as strong as their confidence in its truth. So to disciple our kids into a biblical sexual worldview, they first need to know God's original design. We can't be content with giving our kids bits and pieces of the picture. They need to see the whole enchilada—the full picture created by the Christian worldview—so they can begin piecing their worldview together as they grow and learn.

Mama Bear Apologetics Guide to Sexuality, page 39

ACTIVE READING NOTES

READING FOCUS	MY RESPONSE
Before You Read:	
After skimming the chapter title and subheads, what is one question you would like to have answered in the chapter?	My question:
While You Read:	
Vocabulary List three words you found in the chapter in addition to the words we have provided.	My words: Book words: *metaphysical* (page 37) — *teleology* (page 42) — *telos* (page 42) —
After You Read:	
Answer Did you find an answer to your pre-reading question? (We hope so.) If yes, write it down.	My answer:

"Aha!" moments	My "Aha!" moments:
List three things you highlighted or underlined in the chapter. This can be new information you learned, encouraging reinforcements of things you already knew, or just plain anything that popped out at you.	1. 2. 3.

PICK A QUESTION

Use this space to review the study questions at the end of the chapter and respond to the one you find most thought-provoking or convicting.

EMPOWERING WORDS

- *Epistemology*—This is the study of how we gain knowledge. It engages questions like, "What is knowledge?" and "How is knowledge acquired?"

- *Moral relativism*—This idea suggests there is no universal or absolute set of moral principles, but that moral standards are defined by people according to their time, place, and context, and cannot be objectively determined.

- *General revelation*—This refers to the truths that can be known about God through His creation.

- *Special revelation*—God has chosen to reveal Himself through miraculous means, including the written Word of God, and, most importantly, Jesus Christ.

- *Justification*—This is the legal act of God in which He considers our sins forgiven and applies Christ's righteousness to us.

- *Glorification*—When Christ returns and gives all believers—alive and dead—perfect resurrected bodies like His own, we will be glorified.

EMPOWERING THOUGHTS

In this chapter we learn how to understand a worldview by looking at several analogies. Look through the four analogies discussed on pages 37-39, and record what each analogy teaches about the significance and function of a worldview by answering the following questions:

A WORLDVIEW IS LIKE...(ANALOGY)	WORLDVIEW FUNCTION
Rules to a Game	How is a worldview like the rules to a game?
A Lens	How does a well-oriented worldview help us see accurately?
A Filter	What should a good worldview allow in and keep out?

A Puzzle Box Top	How does knowing what a biblical worldview is supposed to look like help our kids?

 ### Your Worldview Puzzle

Do the unthinkable and mix up two puzzles in one box. Tell your kids that some of the pieces from another puzzle made their way into the box. As you put the puzzle together with them, listen to the ways they figure out which puzzle pieces belong and which don't. (You're going to ask them to recall what they said later, but jot down notes in case they forget.) Use this as a starting point by asking your kids:

- How did looking at the whole box top help them know which pieces went to their puzzle and which didn't?

- How did they feel when they encountered pieces from the other puzzle? Frustrated? Wish they weren't there? Triumphant when they figured it out?

- What did they do with the pieces from another puzzle? Put them in a separate place? What did they do with the pieces they weren't sure about? Another spot? Did they ever reject a piece and then have to go looking for it?

- Discuss how the process is the same with Christianity. God has given us His Word, which helps us know which ideological pieces to accept into our worldview and which are not part of His original plan. The world has its own puzzle (worldview) it is trying to promote.

Fully understanding the biblical worldview helps us distinguish when an unbiblical idea is trying to sneak into God's puzzle.

DIGGING DEEPER

1. Take a look at the questions a worldview answers as listed on page 37-38. How do the answers to these questions change depending on whether God or humans are the foundation of truth and reality?

WORLDVIEW QUESTIONS	GOD AS THE FOUNDATION	HUMANS AS THE FOUNDATION
What constitutes reality?		
Does objective truth exist?		
How do we discover truth?		
What counts as "good"?		
What counts as "evil"?		
Where did we come from?		

What is our ultimate destiny?		
What does it mean to be human?		
What is our purpose in this life?		

2. On page 42 (section 4), we read, "Everything goes screwy when people don't understand the purpose for which they were created."

   a. Illustrate this claim by creating an analogy using a common household appliance or gadget.

   b. List one or two counterfeit (unbiblical) purposes for humanity you've seen promoted in our culture.

3. On page 42 (section 5), we read, "Walking within God's boundaries allows us to live in harmony with Him. And since Christians believe that the eternal moral laws stem from an eternal, moral law giver, then we believe that following His commands will lead us to a life of flourishing."

a. What messages have you heard from culture about what will lead to fulfillment?

b. If someone asked you to define biblical human flourishing, how would you answer them?

4. Describe the concept of *teleology*.

• What is the *telos* of scissors?

• Of a Crock-Pot?

• Of a duck's webbed feet?

5. A *telos* also determines what is within an organism's nature. Have you ever seen an animal that was not allowed to act like an animal? A dog that was always chained up? A horse that never left a small pen? How do we see flourishing decline even

on the animal level when animals are not allowed to fulfill their *telos*?

6. According to points 4, 5, and 7 on pages 42-44, why would we *expect* a kind of peace when obeying God? How does the truth that not everything is redeemed *yet* (see page 44) prepare us to wage a war against our natural inclinations in order to find this peace? How do these two seemingly contradictory points match what we experience in reality?

7. On page 45, we read, "Our desires don't change the truth; they just reveal our fallenness." Give an example from your own life to illustrate and support this claim.

8. How does understanding the way our bodies were created inform how we treat our bodies? How does *ignoring* the way we were created show disrespect for God as creator?

9. Read pages 45-46 and explain the following statement: *Sexual sin can be a symptom, not the root problem.*

KEY SCRIPTURES

We encourage you to read the following verses in context (meaning, read at least the entire chapter). Reflect on how they relate to what you're learning, and thank God for the hope and guidance found in His Word.

- Colossians 1:17—"He is before all things, and in him all things hold together."

- Acts 17:28—"'In him we live and move and have our being'; as even some of your own poets have said, 'For we are indeed his offspring.'"

- Colossians 2:13—"You, who were dead in your trespasses and the uncircumcision of your flesh, God made alive together with him, having forgiven us all our trespasses."

- Psalm 98:1—"Oh sing to the LORD a new song, for he has done marvelous things! His right hand and his holy arm have worked salvation for him."

PAWS FOR PRAYER

In closing this chapter, reflect on what you learned in lesson 2 and journal your prayer to God here:

Praise:

Admit:

Worship with thanksgiving:

Supplication (ask):

A PRETTY GREAT DESIGN, WHEN FOLLOWED

Gender, sex, marriage, and family were intended to show us the God we can't see. And even more than that, *they point the world to the God whom they cannot see in hopes that what is invisible can become more understandable.* Any movement which seeks to destroy gender, sex, marriage, or family is destroying the message God intended, the picture He gave us in order to understand Him. And that picture is a pretty great design...*when followed.*

Mama Bear Apologetics Guide to Sexuality, pages 64-65

ACTIVE READING NOTES

READING FOCUS	MY RESPONSE
Before You Read:	
After skimming the chapter title and subheads, what is one question you would like to have answered in the chapter?	My question:
While You Read:	
Vocabulary List three words you found in the chapter in addition to the words we have provided.	My words: Book words: *ontology* (page 54)— *functional hierarchy* (page 54)— *imago dei* (page 58)—
After You Read:	
Answer Did you find an answer to your pre-reading question? (We hope so.) If yes, write it down.	My answer:

"Aha!" moments	My "Aha!" moments:
List three things you highlighted or underlined in the chapter. This can be new information you learned, encouraging reinforcements of things you already knew, or just plain anything that popped out at you.	1. 2. 3.

PICK A QUESTION

Use this space to review the study questions at the end of the chapter and respond to the one you find most thought-provoking or convicting.

EMPOWERING WORDS

- *Communicable attributes of God*—Some characteristics of God's nature are imparted to believers, such as faithfulness, truthfulness, mercy, goodness, justice, love, grace, and holiness.

- *Incommunicable attributes of God*—God also has unique characteristics, such as immutability, eternality, omnipresence, omniscience, and aseity (self-origination).

- *Covenant*—A sacred, unchangeable, and binding agreement exists between God and humanity that stipulates the conditions of their relationship.

- *Union with Christ*—We receive all the benefits of salvation because of the relationship between believers and

Christ. We are in Christ, and He is in us. We are with Christ and becoming like Christ.

- *Subordinationism*—the heresy which states that the Son is ontologically *inferior* to the Father (not to be confused with the historic biblical teaching that the Son is *functionally* subordinate to the Father).

EMPOWERING THOUGHTS

One skeptical claim against the existence of God goes something like this: "No hide-and-seek game lasts this long." The assertion is that if God exists, there's no way to know because He is and always has been completely hidden and silent.

Scripture tells another story. Romans 1:20 (NIV) tells us, "Since the creation of the world God's invisible qualities—his eternal power and divine nature—have been clearly seen, being understood from what has been made, so that people are without excuse."

Does this sound like a hide-and-seek game? In fact, it seems like God's revealed quite a bit about His existence and nature in the things He has made. In this chapter, we learn about several messages God sends through the "things that have been made," namely gender, marriage, sex, and family.

1. In the space below, summarize in one or two sentences the message God intends to send through each of those:

   a. The message of gender (pages 58-59)—

   b. The message of marriage (pages 59-60)—

c. The message of sex (pages 60-61)—

d. The message of family (pages 61-62)—

Each message reflects a picture. For example, the message of gender paints a picture of the image of God. In the space below, describe how secularism has warped each message. What might be the ramifications of these warped worldviews on our human understanding of God? (Feel free to get creative here.)

2. The secular message of gender: Gender is just_____

_____.

If taken as a picture of God, this understanding depicts God as

_____

_____.

3. The secular message of marriage: Marriage is just_____

_____.

If taken as a picture of God, this understanding depicts God as

_____

_____.

4. The secular message of sex: Sex is just _____

   _____.

   If taken as a picture of God, this understanding depicts God as

   _____

   _____.

5. The secular message of family: Family is just _____

   _____.

   If taken as a picture of God, this understanding depicts God as

   _____

   _____.

DIGGING DEEPER

1. In this chapter we touch on biblical authority and address some of the perversions and broken examples that hinder our submission to God's design. On page 50, we learn that willing and even joyful submission to God's design is possible when we understand God's goodness, trusting in His love.

   a. How might those with broken examples of authority overcome past trauma and learn to trust in God's goodness?

   b. Jesus teaches that He is the exact representation of the Father (John 14:9). What can we learn about God's heart through Jesus in the following verses?

- Matthew 8:1-4

- Matthew 9:9-13

- Matthew 11:28-30

2. What kind of authority figures have you experienced in your own life? Were they easy or hard to follow? Have you ever noticed yourself interacting with God in a similar way as you interacted with your earthly authority figures?

3. What is the difference between *functional* hierarchy and *ontological* hierarchy? Give examples.

4. Read pages 55-56. How do we see functional hierarchy modeled within the Godhead and what makes it function so smoothly?

5. Review the passage on authority within the Godhead on pages 54-56. How do we see functional hierarchy (sometimes called functional order) modeled within the Godhead, and what makes it function so smoothly (page 56)?

6. In our fallen world, how have you seen authority and submission warped to imply inequality between parties? Is that how the Bible views authority? How has this misunderstanding affected the way some men have treated their wives?

7. On page 63, we read, "Like all things, we need balance. We cannot elevate God's good design to the point where people who have missed it feel like they are forever on the outs. And we cannot elevate God's redemption to the point where people feel like there's a get-out-of-jail-free card whenever things get tough."

Almost everyone has a tendency to emphasize one trait over the other—God's wrath and God's love, God's design and God's redemption. Which characteristics do you gravitate toward?

8. On page 63, we read, "We cannot stop lifting up God's design as the ideal, even if we haven't attained it."

   a. Why is this true?

   b. Consider a coach, leader, or teacher who is able to influence and lead others to excellence despite his or her own imperfections. How can this example encourage us to lovingly reinforce God's design with our children even if we have fallen short in our own lives?

 ## The Importance of Original Design

If you have access, watch an episode of the reality TV show *Nailed It!* How closely did the contestants adhere to the original? Could someone recreate the original from looking at the contestants' cobbled-together, hurried versions? Why is always understanding the original design important for recreating it? Ask your kids if they can explain God's design for people.

9. On page 64, we read, "Family is the first institution created by God. Almost everything that can be known about God was *intended* to be known within the context of family."

List three things you believe can be known about God's heart, plans, or ways within the context of family as God designed it.

- • _____

- • _____

- • _____

KEY SCRIPTURES

We encourage you to read the following verses in context (meaning, read at least the entire chapter). Reflect on how they relate to what you're learning, and thank God for the hope and guidance found in His Word.

- • Romans 2:4—"Do you presume on the riches of his kindness and forbearance and patience, not knowing that God's kindness is meant to lead you to repentance?"

- • Hebrews 4:16—"Let us then with confidence draw near to the throne of grace, that we may receive mercy and find grace to help in time of need."

- • 1 Corinthians 10:31—"Whether you eat or drink, or whatever you do, do all to the glory of God."

- • Ecclesiastes 12:13—"The end of the matter; all has been heard. Fear God and keep his commandments, for this is the whole duty of man."

PAWS FOR PRAYER

In closing this chapter, reflect on what you learned in lesson 3 and journal your prayer to God here:

Praise:

Admit:

Worship with thanksgiving:

Supplication (ask):

LESSON 4

DEMOLISHING ARGUMENTS, NOT PEOPLE

Jesus dealt with ideas forcefully and without apology. He also dealt with individuals according to their need: what was keeping the person from unifying with the heart and mind of God? We should model our approach after Jesus. We don't just answer questions, we answer *people*. There is a time to demolish arguments and a time to love a person tangled in a thorn bush of bad ideas. Ultimately, we need to teach our kids how to do both.

Mama Bear Apologetics Guide to Sexuality, page 78

ACTIVE READING NOTES

READING FOCUS	MY RESPONSE
Before You Read:	
After skimming the chapter title and subheads, what is one question you would like to have answered in the chapter?	My question:
While You Read:	
Vocabulary List three words you found in the chapter in addition to the words we have provided.	My words: Book words: *deductive reasoning* (page 72)— *incoherent* (page 73)— *grounding problem* (page 74)— *emotional reasoning* (page 74)—

After You Read:	
Answer Did you find an answer to your pre-reading question? (We hope so.) If yes, write it down.	My answer:
"Aha!" moments List three things you highlighted or underlined in the chapter. This can be new information you learned, encouraging reinforcements of things you already knew, or just plain anything that popped out at you.	My "Aha!" moments: 1. 2. 3.

PICK A QUESTION

Use this space to review the study questions at the end of the chapter and respond to the one you find most thought-provoking or convicting.

EMPOWERING WORDS

- *Emotionalism*—Prioritizing our feelings over our God-given reasoning faculties is choosing emotionalism.

- *Judgment*—Judgment is assessing a situation and drawing conclusions based on one's perception of truth/reality.

- *Reason*—We've been given this ability of the mind to

think, understand, and support thoughts and conclusions through logic.

- *Hermeneutics*—The study of the principles and methods of interpreting the biblical text.

- *Grounding problem*—If you accept a concept without a bedrock truth to support it, then you have a grounding problem. For example, could someone or something have an intentional and purposeful design without a designer?

Playing the Image of God Game: Image Bearers Versus Image Reflectors

Your children know they're special; they know they were created in the image of God. Now, your job is to show them that *every* person is a fellow image-bearer! Whenever you're out and about, or whenever you're talking about another person, make sure to ask, "Is that person made in the image of God?" (Don't forget to add questions about things *not* in the image of God—a cute puppy, a really good candy bar, a squirrel. Fabulous as those are, they are not created in the image of God the way humans are.) Maybe the person has differently colored hair or skin from your family. Maybe he's differently abled, or maybe she's dressed like a clown. Maybe it's a baby in the womb! No matter how that person looks or acts, remind your kids that *all* humans are created in the image of God and are thus worthy of dignity and respect.

Once the category "made in the image of God" is firmly connected to all humans, let's get a little more nuanced. Create in their mind a second category: "actions that do or do not reflect the image of God." As humans we are all *created* in God's image, but we can make decisions that do not *reflect* His image. Did a person's theft reflect God's image? No. Was the person who cussed at them on the highway reflecting God's image? No. Even when you discipline your kids, remind them, "This does not change your standing as an image-bearer of God. However, your actions did not reflect that image, so there will be consequences for your behavior." This makes the category personal, showing how even they—your darlings—can poorly reflect God's image. Yet no matter their behavior, nothing can change their identity as image-bearers of God.

As you have this conversation day after day, year after year, it will be easier to introduce societal behaviors (especially those pertaining to sexuality) that do not reflect God's design. Children will already know that a person's actions have no bearing on whether the individual is made in the image of God and worthy of dignity and respect. They will be able to distinguish between *identity* and *behavior*. Remind them that while some people choose to identify themselves by their behavior, that is not how we as Christians will identify them.

EMPOWERING THOUGHTS

God didn't create people because He needs us. He created us because He *desires* us. He wanted image-bearers with whom He could dwell, to whom He could pour out all His love, and with whom He could reign. And yes, we will reign with Him! It was His plan in the first chapter of the Bible, and it's *still* His plan in the last (Genesis 1:26 and Revelation 22:5). He wanted relationship with us, and He's gone to great lengths to secure an eternal relationship for any who'll have Him.

Since relationship is immensely important to God, relationship should be important to us. And as we wade into the deep waters of discussions related to human sexuality, we will frequently be confronted with the question, "Would you rather be right or have relationship?" This doesn't mean we can't have both. But it does mean that if we aren't careful, we could walk away from a discussion having won an argument but having lost future opportunities to show Christ's love because our relational bridge has been burned. If the victim of our victory ever needs a compassionate ear or friendly guidance in the future, our phone won't be ringing.

In the main book's chapter, we look at four categories that can help us to approach and love people well, maintaining relationship without compromising truth. Share a personal takeaway from each category below:

1. Is This a Person or an Idea? (page 69)

_____

2. An Enemy with No Scruples (pages 69-72)

_____

3. Loving God by Loving Truth (pages 72-76)

_____

4. Embracing Our Inner Warrior Bear and Nurturing Bear (pages 76-78)

_____

A common parenting maxim is: "Rules without relationship lead to rebellion." What can we learn about God from this picture of parenting? How have you experienced the truth of this statement in your own life?

 RESPONDING TO PEOPLE

Everyone's had experience with a really rude person. It could be a kid at school, a waiter at a restaurant, or another customer at a grocery store. Rudeness should never be excused, but it can be explained given further context. How would your response to the person be different if you knew they had just experienced a death in the family? Had just come from a class where the teacher berated them in front of the whole group? Just declared bankruptcy? Next time you find yourself in a situation where a person has behaved inappropriately, wait until you and the kids are alone and imagine possible situations that might have contributed to that person's bad attitude—situations which help elicit compassion on our end. How can getting outside our own experience of a situation help us to treat others with the dignity and respect as image-bearers even when they don't reflect His image?

DIGGING DEEPER

1. Describe how today's cultural sexual ideologies are like getting caught in a thorn bush.

2. How does a false definition of love (i.e. celebrating every person's gender or sexual preference) damage a person's Christian worldview? (pages 70-71)

3. What is the proper way to love God and love others? (pages 71-72)

4. Why do you think truth is so necessary for biblical love (and a biblical worldview)? (John 4:24, John 14:6, 1 John 4:8)

5. If God (the Divine Mind) doesn't exist, not only is human life purposeless, but it's objectively worthless. Think of one or two other human values that suffer the "grounding problem" without God. (See pages 73-74.)

- _____

- _____

6. Read pages 72-76 on logical and emotional reasoning and then go to https://mamabearapologetics.com/logic-worksheet/ to download the worksheet. See if you can do a few of the logic questions. What is the main difference between *logical* reasoning and *emotional* reasoning? (Hint: emotional reasoning has a universal assumption of what?)

7. Jesus spoke boldly to crowds and boldly to individuals. What was the difference in His approach?

How can you apply His example to your own life?

 When Needs Affect Behaviors

Consider the times when your kids act out in disobedience. Sometimes their behavior is simply rebellion, but sometimes it stems from an unmet need or simply being exhausted at the end of a hard day. Consequences should always follow inappropriate behavior, but sometimes the deeper needs ought to be addressed first. Is your daughter overwhelmed by outside stimuli? Maybe she needs a bubble bath before you discuss the consequences of her actions. Is your son acting out of frustration over a social or family situation? Sometimes healthy comfort food will help him relax enough to discuss his actions. In both these examples, we are addressing our children's deeper needs with grace before launching into correction mode.

KEY SCRIPTURES

We encourage you to read the following verses in context (meaning, read at least the entire chapter). Reflect on how they relate to what you're learning, and thank God for the hope and guidance found in His Word.

- Mark 10:27— "With man it is impossible, but not with God. For all things are possible with God."

- John 14:15— "If you love me, you will keep my commandments."

- Hebrews 10:17— "I will remember their sins and their lawless deeds no more."

- Matthew 10:34— "Do not think that I have come to bring peace to the earth. I have not come to bring peace, but a sword."

 Learn the "Prayer of Saint Francis" with your children.

Lord, make me an instrument of Your peace.
Where there is hatred, let me sow love.
Where there is injury, let me bring pardon.
Where there is doubt, let me bring faith.
Where there is despair, let me bring hope.
Where there is darkness, let me bring Your light.
Where there is sadness, let me bring joy.
O divine Master, let me not seek as much
to be consoled as to console,
to be understood as to understand,
to be loved as to love,
for it is in giving that we receive,
it is in pardoning that we are pardoned,
and it is in dying that we are born to everlasting life.

PAWS FOR PRAYER

In closing this chapter, reflect on what you learned in lesson 4 and journal your prayer to God here:

Praise:

Admit:

Worship with thanksgiving:

Supplication (ask):

Part Two

WAIT, MY KIDS ARE BEING TAUGHT WHAT?!

Aworldview is the lens through which you perceive the world around you. It affects how you interpret your lived experiences and how you draw conclusions about how the world works. It influences what you do with all the puzzle pieces life throws your way and how you answer life's most significant questions: What does it mean to be human? Why are we here? Where did we come from? What is wrong with the world? How can it be fixed? Where are we headed? What is true "human flourishing"?

The biblical worldview is both cohesive and in line with reality. It stands apart from others in that—when properly understood—it can be applied to life's big questions. The biblical worldview does not contradict itself, and it results in a society that is orderly and safe. It also results in hope, peace, and objectively verifiable answers.

In part two, we will learn about the unbiblical worldview that is guiding the mission and values behind some of the confusing and dangerous sexual guidelines influencing public education and secular thought today. We will witness *linguistic theft* at work again as we look beneath the surface of the sexual agenda that seeks to tempt our kids with nice-sounding concepts, subtly (and sometimes not so subtly) pulling them outside the God-glorifying boundaries intended to protect and bless them.

This section offers several practical steps parents can take toward greater awareness and advice on how to be salt and light to our local government, schools, and communities as we walk in respect while not compromising on truth.

LESSON 5

ARE YOU SEX SMARTER THAN A FIFTH GRADER?

Experimenting with different genders and different sexual orientations is apparently a "normal" part of sexual development. To this I have to ask, "How did *we* all turn out okay? Were we all doing it wrong up until now?"...Our kids are seeking what we all sought back when we were young—a way to fit in and be accepted. They used to want to grow up to be firefighters and astronauts because that is who our society lauded as heroes. Today, there is a virtual parade of new "heroes" whose only claim to fame is who they sleep with or what has changed between their legs. Declaring oneself to be a sexual minority is not just accepted but celebrated, and our kids are interpreting it as the fastest fast-track ever to celebrity.

Mama Bear Apologetics Guide to Sexuality, pages 84, 97

ACTIVE READING NOTES

READING FOCUS	MY RESPONSE
Before You Read:	
After skimming the chapter title and subheads, what is one question you would like to have answered in the chapter?	My question:
While You Read:	
Vocabulary List three words you found in the chapter in addition to the words we have provided.	My words: Book words: *NSES* (page 83)— *sexual risk avoidance* (page 85)— *sexual risk reduction* (page 85)— *sexual autonomy* (page 87)— *marginalize* (page 91)—

After You Read:	
Answer Did you find an answer to your pre-reading question? (We hope so.) If yes, write it down.	My answer:
"Aha!" moments List three things you highlighted or underlined in the chapter. This can be new information you learned, encouraging reinforcements of things you already knew, or just plain anything that popped out at you.	My "Aha!" moments: 1. 2. 3.

PICK A QUESTION

Use this space to review the study questions at the end of the chapter and respond to the one you find most thought-provoking or convicting.

EMPOWERING WORDS

- *Ontology*—In simple terms, this branch of philosophy seeks the classification and explanation of essence, being, and existence.

- *Sociology*—Sociology is the study of the development, structure, and functioning of human society and social problems.

- *Anthropology*—This is the study of humanity through the application of biology, cultural studies, archaeology, linguistics, and other social sciences.

- *Theology*—Theology is study of the nature of God.

- *Remnant*—God has always reserved for Himself a group of people who are faithful in deed, not just in word, no matter how culture changes around them. This doctrine says they will ultimately experience the fulfillment of God's promises (1 Kings 19:18; Zephaniah 3:9-20; Revelation 12:17).

EMPOWERING THOUGHTS

The Christian worldview helps us understand and accept the reality that we see around us—both the good and bad—while at the same time explaining why we intuitively know that things are not the way they are supposed to be. One of the most important parts of the Christian worldview is our view of eternal life and the fact that this world is not our true home! All the injustices, all the suffering, all the crime, all the unhealthiness, will ultimately be dealt with, *and not by us.* By following the commands of Jesus, we create little ripples around us which point to the kingdom that will one day be our home. But we are not responsible for making the entire world a utopian reality in the here and now. We live at the nexus of freedom and empowerment; freedom to rest in God's sovereignty while—at the same time—being empowered to cultivate the environment around us for the glory of God. Selah, y'all.

 From Fun to Anarchy in Less Than an Hour

Grab a board game or a card game your family plays frequently. Tell your kids that there's a new rule: This time, *anyone* can make *any* new rule, *whenever* they want. For instance, if yellow's about to win, blue can declare that blue is now allowed to switch places with any other player on the board. It might start out with laughter, but be sure to step in before your children throttle each other.

Once you're finished playing, ask your kids: How much harder was it to play the game? While it might have been fun for a little while to make up the rules, did the fun last? Use this as an illustration for your kids about why we need rules that don't change, and why they should come from an outside party (like God). Because anyone *in* the game is trying to change the rules *in their own favor.*

DIGGING DEEPER

1. In this chapter we are introduced to the National Sex Education Standards (NSES) coming to a school near you. On page 85, we learn what steps we can take to become more informed and engaged in what's going on at a local level. In the space below, describe each of those steps:

    Step One: Gather _____

    _____

    Step Two: Contact _____

    _____

    Step Three: Find out _____

    _____

    Step Four: Ask _____

    _____

2. If, after researching, we have objections, what is the proper chain of communication we should try to follow (pages 85-86)? Answer on the next page.

First contact: _____

Second contact: _____

Third contact: _____

Fourth contact: _____

3. Why should we keep good records and paper trails of our conversations?

And remember, our actions can speak louder than words. We want to be salt and light.

4. Have you ever brought an objection to one of your children's teachers (maybe even at church)? In what ways did you use grace, and in what ways did you use discernment?

5. What are some things you can do today to build a relational bridge with the teachers, principals, and schoolboards in your community?

6. What three factors make up a "healthy" relationship according to the NSES (page 87)?

   - _____

   - _____

   - _____

7. From the perspective of sex-positivity, the goal is to help kids become familiar with their sexual identity by way of exploring all the options (page 84).

   a. What is God's goal for our children's sexuality? See 1 Thessalonians 4:3-5.

   b. What does the Bible say about our wants? See Colossians 3:5.

   c. What does the Bible say about our needs? See Matthew 6:25-34.

   d. Not all explorations end well. List at least two potentially life-altering consequences of sexual exploration.

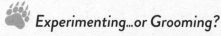 *Experimenting...or Grooming?*

If your kids are older, discuss the NSES's presumption that they can learn about their sexual identity by experimenting with all the options. In the main book, maxim #15 (page 252) reminds us that through neuroplasticity, people can train their brains what to crave. If this is true, how might experimenting with sexuality outside God's design actually lead them to *prefer* an unbiblical sexuality because they have now practiced or normalized it? Do your kids think it would be harder or easier to return to God's design after creating these new neural pathways? Why?

You can also start creating this paradigm for younger kids. If you go out for ice cream, ask, "Who do you think craves ice cream more—the person who eats it once a week or the person who eats it every night?" Or if your kids are struggling to get along, ask, "Who has a harder time not hitting their siblings—the kid who tries to be kind or the kid who hits her brother every day?" Explain that we train our bodies to crave certain foods and actions through our behaviors.

8. On pages 90-91, we are introduced to Queer Theory and its claims about language. According to this theory, words are not just information. They are also a means of _____ _____.

9. Queer theorists believe words are social constructs used by the oppressor class to marginalize people groups. Queer theorists also believe that gender is a social construct independent of biology, and "if society made the two-gender rule, they can make the 58-gender rule" (page 91).

According to this theory, how are words being used as a form of oppression?

10. As a worldview, Marxism rarely shows up the same way twice, cropping up in new and inventive ways trying to infect us with unbiblical beliefs. Constant through the changes in appearance, however, is (1) the dividing of people into groups and then pitting them against one another and (2) the progressive push toward freedom from sexual repression and oppression. While many of us are seeing the ugly fruit of these ideas influencing our children in new and alarming ways, the seeds were planted long ago. In the space below, summarize the three main assumptions of a Marxist worldview from pages 91-94:

Assumption 1: _____

_____

Assumption 2: _____

_____

Assumption 3: _____

_____

11. Marxism answers many of the same questions the Christian worldview answers, albeit very differently. Refer to pages 93-94 to complete the chart and compare:

QUESTION	MARXISM'S ANSWER	CHRISTIANITY'S ANSWER
Why are we here?		
What is morality?		
What is wrong with the world?		
How are we redeemed from what is wrong with the world?		

12. Reflect on the differences between the answers. How have you seen the Marxist worldview at work in our culture?

13. Look at the "Matrix of Oppression" at the top of page 95.

a. Define yourself according to this matrix:

b. How does this identity compare to your identity in Christ? (Galatians 3:28)

c. Teaching our kids to defend individuals who are experiencing mistreatment is different from teaching them to defend entire classes of people. Why is this an important distinction? (page 96)

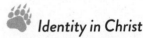 **Identity in Christ**

Talk to your kids about different jobs and the personality traits and roles that are included with the job description. What are some of the requirements of a teacher, and what personal qualities make them effective at their job? How about a nurse? Computer programmer? If we were to create a "job description" for a Christian, what might that look like? What are some of the roles and requirements of a Christian? (You might mention being salt and light, taking up your cross, loving God and others, and obeying the Lord's commands.) What are some traits we should be committed to embodying? (Hint: Check out Galatians 5:22-23.) How should our everyday decisions flow from being a disciple of Jesus Christ? How can this primary identity inform the way we live in the world?

KEY SCRIPTURES

We encourage you to read the following verses in context (meaning, read at least the entire chapter). Reflect on how they relate to what you're learning, and thank God for the hope and guidance found in His Word.

- Matthew 5:16—"In the same way, let your light shine before others, so that they may see your good works and give glory to your Father who is in heaven."

- Romans 13:1—"Let every person be subject to the governing authorities. For there is no authority except from God, and those that exist have been instituted by God."

- 2 Timothy 4:3-4—"The time is coming when people will not endure sound teaching, but having itching ears they will accumulate for themselves teachers to suit their own passions, and will turn away from listening to the truth and wander off into myths."

PAWS FOR PRAYER

In closing this chapter, reflect on what you learned in lesson 5 and journal your prayer to God here:

Praise:

Admit:

Worship with thanksgiving:

Supplication (ask):

LESSON 6

THE ENEMY'S NEW PLAYBOOK

If the enemy wants to thwart humans and God from coming into right relationship again, he can go after their individual identities. That's what we saw happen in the garden, that's what we saw when Satan attacked Christ here on earth, and that's what we are seeing happening now.

So how is he attacking identity? Let's go back a step and think about what is required to even *have* a true identity. At minimum, you need two things: truth and words. You cannot *have* a true identity without the concept of truth, and you cannot *convey* a true identity apart from the use of words. Destroy truth and words, and you can destroy our ability to communicate true identities, which in turn impedes our ability to communicate the gospel.

Mama Bear Apologetics Guide to Sexuality, page 105

ACTIVE READING NOTES

READING FOCUS	MY RESPONSE
Before You Read:	
After skimming the chapter title and subheads, what is one question you would like to have answered in the chapter?	My question:
While You Read:	
Vocabulary Here you will list three words you found in the chapter, and we will add a few words we want to make sure you find.	My words: Book words: *semantic shift* (page 106)— *linguistic theft* (page 106)— *categorical words* (page 106)— *linguistic smuggling* (page 107)—
After You Read:	
Answer Did you find an answer to your pre-reading question? (We hope so.) If yes, write it down.	My answer:

"Aha!" Moments	My "Aha!" moments:
List three things you highlighted or underlined in the chapter. This can be new information you learned, encouraging reinforcements of things you already knew, or just plain anything that popped out at you.	1. 2. 3.

PICK A QUESTION

Use this space to review the study questions at the end of the chapter and respond to the one you find most thought-provoking or convicting.

EMPOWERING WORDS

- *Denotation*—The dictionary definition or primary meaning of a word is its denotation, in contrast to the feelings or ideas that the word suggests.

- *Connotation*—If a word invokes positive or negative feelings in addition to its literal or primary meaning, those are its connotations.

- *Category error (or mistake)*—A category error is a semantic or ontological error by which a property is ascribed to a thing that could not possibly have that property. For example, "The number two is blue."

EMPOWERING THOUGHTS

One popular postmodern approach to words is to declare that

words are meaningless. They're just made up, useful fictions, and we can't really pin them down to any singular meaning. True, there are different words in different languages that may mean the same thing, so in that sense they are "made up." But words are very powerful because they *refer to real things*. Words are how we interact with reality. Words are so important that in John 1:1, Jesus Himself is referred to as *the Word*. So, if your kids come to you with this line of argument (as one of our Mama Bear's children recently did), help them clarify their thoughts—"So, I hear you *using words* to describe how words are meaningless. Is that right?"—and then use their own "logic" to reinforce how important words are in the real world. You might say, "What I just heard you say was that you are going to come home after school and clean the whole kitchen, do the dishes, and wash the dog. If words are made up, then I'm free to interpret your words any way I want, right? Thanks!"

All this goes to show that when you deviate from a Christian worldview, chaos is not far behind. Properly understood and applied, the biblical worldview is the foundation of an orderly and coherent world. Just for fun, brainstorm what you think would happen to our world if everyone woke up and decided that words were meaningless. What parts of society would crumble or cease to function?

Category or Information?

Look at the following categorical statements with your children. Beneath each, write a scenario that would provide actual information that would make the statement true. This might give you an opportunity to correct your children in their categories! Maybe they say, "My teacher always gives me a bad grade." Does this mean the teacher hates them? Not necessarily, and especially not if we are talking about math! Keep statements like these in mind when your kids are telling you about their day. Regularly help them articulate objective statements rather than categories.

STATEMENT	ACTION WHICH WOULD MAKE THE STATEMENT TRUE
My teacher hates me!	
Aidan is such a bully.	
You're always so selfish.	
I can't trust Allison.	

Please note: If a person or a situation is making your child uncomfortable, he or she might not be able to articulate why. Sometimes, it's best to listen to our gut. That's perfectly fine! But this exercise can help children build the muscle of articulating their perceptions and conclusions.

1. Read the last paragraph on page 107. Explain what can happen to children who have been raised to respect authority when words are smuggled into incorrect categories.

The Straw Man fallacy is a logical error in which someone creates a parody of their opponent's position, exaggerating it in such a way that no reasonable person could agree with it. This makes it easier to refute.

2. As an example, how do the pro-life and pro-choice movements mischaracterize each other's positions?

3. Where else have you seen Straw Man arguments constructed?

4. Do you think the church is innocent of this? Why or why not?

DIGGING DEEPER

1. In your own words, explain the tactic of moralizing evil (page 102).

2. Can you give an example of moralizing evil from a popular movie? How does it put a positive spin on an action or attitude that would not normally be condoned by Christians?

3. Repetition in and of itself is not good or bad (page 103).

   List two positive outcomes of repetition from your own life:

   List two negative outcomes of repetition from your own life:

4. After reading pages 104-106, explain the war on words. What is needed in order to have a true identity, and why does messing with the identity of humans and God have an impact on our ability to communicate the gospel?

 The Power of Positive Repetition

Consider an area in which your child is struggling. What is a *truthful* statement (that is, don't tell him he's great at something if he's not) that you can speak over him to encourage him? Repeat your encouragement every day—even multiple times a day if it feels natural. Do this for at least a week. Do you see any difference in your child's attitude regarding their struggle? What does this show us about the importance of positive repetition?

5. Linguistic theft and smuggling are effective tactics of the enemy for a variety of reasons. List four reasons given in the chapter (pages 108-109):

- _____

- _____

- _____

- _____

6. Describe a time when you or your children witnessed one of the consequences of the enemy's tactics listed above:

7. Fill in the blanks from the section on stolen words (pages 109-112):

- *Harm*—We must remind our children that something can _____ without _____.

- *Injustice*—Our world treats _____ as synonymous with _____. If anything is _____, then it is _____.

- *Marriage*—While different forms of marriage are _____ in Scripture (usually multiple wives), that is not God's _____ of marriage.

- *Power, Authority, and Oppression*—Just because _____
  authorities exist doesn't mean that _____ itself
  is bad.

KEY SCRIPTURES

We encourage you to read the following verses in context (read at least the entire chapter), reflect on how they relate to what you're learning, and thank God for the hope and guidance found in His Word.

- Deuteronomy 32:4—"The Rock, his work is perfect, for all his ways are justice. A God of faithfulness and without iniquity, just and upright is he."

- Romans 12:21—"Do not be overcome by evil, but overcome evil with good."

- 3 John 11—"Beloved, do not imitate evil but imitate good. Whoever does good is from God; whoever does evil has not seen God."

- Exodus 32:5—"Aaron...built an altar before [the calf]. And Aaron made a proclamation and said, 'Tomorrow shall be a feast to the LORD.'"

- 1 John 3:18—"Little children, let us not love in word or talk but in deed and in truth."

PAWS FOR PRAYER

In closing this chapter, reflect on what you learned in lesson 6 and journal your prayer to God here:

Praise:

Admit:

Worship with thanksgiving:

Supplication (ask):

LESSON 7

THE GENDERBREAD PERSON

Friends, we were created by God for relationship, and healthy relationships include an emotional component. What has happened to our understanding of healthy, platonic, same-sex friendship? If our kids are buying into the propaganda that a desire for an emotional attachment with someone of the same sex means that they have a same-sex sexual orientation, then be prepared for a lot of confusion. Healthy relationships begin with healthy same-sex friendships. We cannot take a normal desire and make it a predictor of sexual identity. By this definition, everyone is romantically attracted to their best friends.

Mama Bear Apologetics Guide to Sexuality, page 125

ACTIVE READING NOTES

READING FOCUS	MY RESPONSE
Before You Read:	
After skimming the chapter title and subheads, what is one question you would like to have answered in the chapter?	My question:
While You Read:	
Vocabulary List three words you found in the chapter in addition to the words we have provided.	My words: Book words: *law of identity* (page 116) —
After You Read:	
Answer Did you find an answer to your pre-reading question? (We hope so.) If yes, write it down.	My answer:
"Aha!" moments List three things you highlighted or underlined in the chapter. This can be new information you learned, encouraging reinforcements of things you already knew, or just plain anything that popped out at you.	My "Aha!" moments: 1. 2. 3.

PICK A QUESTION

Use this space to review the study questions at the end of the chapter and respond to the one you find most thought-provoking or convicting.

EMPOWERING WORDS

- *Pedagogy*—Pedagogy is the study of teaching methods, instructional approaches, and theories informing how students learn.

- *Law of non-contradiction*—This foundational principle of logic states that contradictory propositions cannot both be true in the same sense at the same time. For example, an animal cannot be a dog and not a dog at the same time in the same sense.

- *False dichotomy*—When two options are falsely presented as the only two options, they create a false dichotomy. For example, "You either accept my identity or you don't love me."

EMPOWERING THOUGHTS

While the English language has just one word for love, biblical Greek has four words to describe the different kinds of affection people can experience for one another—*agape, eros, phileo,* and *storge.*

Storge: Family love—the natural and mutual affection between family members.

Phileo: Friendship—an emotional connection going deeper than casual acquaintance.

Eros: Romantic love—feelings of sexual attraction and desire.

Agape: Spiritual love—self-sacrificial love that does not require any particular emotions.

 Distinguishing Loves

Regularly talk with your children about the different kinds of love. Be on the lookout for expressions of these loves in culture and in community. When you see friends laughing together (*phileo*), nurses caring for their patients (*agape*), a couple kissing (*eros*), or a family enjoying time together (*storge*), ask your children to identify the type of love they see expressed. Don't be shy about putting the TV on pause and asking this question as y'all watch together. Like the maxims in the main book's afterword, this exercise should be done until your kids want to gag—no, seriously...*until they want to gag*—because our culture is telling your kids that *all* their feelings of attraction are erotic. The more familiar your children are with the different types of love, the less vulnerable they will be to mistaking their own feelings of friendship for those of romance.

DIGGING DEEPER

1. In the book, we learn about the Genderbread Person. Draw your own Genderbread person below and label identity, attraction, expression, and sex.

2. Before reading this book, were you aware of curricula like the Genderbread Person (or Gender Unicorn)? Do you know if these tools are being used in local schools around you?

3. Our lack of awareness has no bearing on something's existence. On page 116, we learn that the Genderbread curriculum is teaching the opposite. Rather than teaching that identity is objectively verifiable (outside of us), students are learning that gender identity is dependent on self-perception (thoughts and feelings). This removes gender from the realm of objective reality to subjective preference or experience. If our children learn that their gender identity is truly a preference based upon feelings (subjective), what other things might they believe to be true about themselves based upon feelings?

4. On page 117, we read, "If our kids think their identity is based on how they identify in the moment, then there is no security in Christ. If they don't *feel* saved, then they aren't. If they don't *feel* like God is close to them at the moment, then He's not. If they *feel* ugly, then they are. Don't try to talk them out of it: The Genderbread Person taught them all about how to determine their identity." What are the consequences of affirming the above examples?

What Makes Me...Me

Ask your children to describe themselves. How do they do it? Is it by their hobbies? Their gender? Their personality traits? Their strengths or weaknesses? Their academic pursuits? What parts of their self-identification can change? What parts will never change?

5. Summarize in 1-2 sentences the Genderbread Person's main takeaway on the following elements:

Identity (pages 116-119):

Expression (pages 119-122):

Sex (pages 122-124):

Attraction (pages 125-127):

6. Read pages 117-118. What are gender stereotypes? In what ways can they be helpful if applied loosely? In what ways can they be damaging if applied too rigidly?

7. Do you think the transgender movement builds up gender stereotypes or breaks them down? Why?

8. What problems do you foresee with defining sexualities if the concept of biological gender has been erased?

9. Without looking at the chapter, see how well you can match each word to its definition. When you're done, refer to the cheat sheet on pages 126-127 and make any corrections in a different colored ink.

VOCABULARY WORD	DEFINITION
A. Homosexual	_____ Being romantically and emotionally attracted (but not necessarily sexually attracted) to someone regardless of the person's gender
B. Lesbian	_____ Not having any sexual attractions, regardless of gender
C. Bisexual	_____Being sexually and/or romantically attracted to people who are trans or androgynous
D. Pansexual	_____ A person sexually attracted to people of the same gender
E. Asexual (or Ace)	_____ A man or a woman sexually attracted to two genders
F. Heteroromantic	_____ Being sexually attracted to all genders
G. Homoromantic	_____ Being romantically and emotionally attracted (but not necessarily sexually attracted) to a person of the opposite gender
H. Panromantic	_____ A woman sexually attracted to women
I. Skoliosexual	_____ Being romantically and emotionally attracted (but not necessarily sexually attracted) to a person of the same gender

10. What other sexual and gender identities have you heard discussed? (For example, *nonbinary* or *gender fluid*)

11. Fill in the blanks (pages 128-129):

    a. We were created by a _____ God for _____, and our families, friendships, and communities give us a picture of the way God relates to us.

    b. We are by nature _____ to _____ things, but _____ for beauty does not equal _____ attraction.

    c. We need to affirm to our kids what kinds of touch are _____ and _____.

    d. Together, we _____ the *imago dei* in a way that _____ and _____ cannot on their own.

KEY SCRIPTURES

We encourage you to read the following verses in context (meaning, read at least the entire chapter). Reflect on how they relate to what you're learning, and thank God for the hope and guidance found in His Word.

- Matthew 7:24—"Everyone then who hears these words of mine and does them will be like a wise man who built his house on the rock."

- Hebrews 13:8—"Jesus Christ is the same yesterday and today and forever."

- Deuteronomy 11:19—"You shall teach [these words] to your children, talking of them when you are sitting in your house, and when you are walking by the way, and when you lie down, and when you rise."

PAWS FOR PRAYER

In closing this chapter, reflect on what you learned in lesson 7 and journal your prayer to God here:

Praise:

Admit:

Worship with thanksgiving:

Supplication (ask):

LESSON 8

SEX-POSITIVITY

The more value something has, the more rules and boundaries we erect to protect it...It's only when something doesn't have any inherent value that you can do whatever you want with it, which turns out to be the skeleton lurking in the closet of sex-positivity. It encourages you to do whatever you want with whomever you want. The implicit message (that most people don't pick up on) is that you and your partner(s) have no inherent value worth protecting. Consent can't provide this value, and neither can pleasure. Sure, sex-positivity may sound like freedom, but in reality, it's saying that your body and what you do with it don't matter.

Mama Bear Apologetics Guide to Sexuality, page 138

ACTIVE READING NOTES

READING FOCUS	MY RESPONSE
Before You Read:	
After skimming the chapter title and subheads, what is one question you would like to have answered in the chapter?	My question:
While You Read:	
Vocabulary List three words you found in the chapter in addition to the words we have provided.	My words: Book words: *death* (page 136)— *moral relativism* (page 136)— *inherent value* (page 138)—
After You Read:	
Answer Did you find an answer to your pre-reading question? (We hope so.) If yes, write it down.	My answer:

"Aha!" moments	My "Aha!" moments:
List three things you highlighted or underlined in the chapter. This can be new information you learned, encouraging reinforcements of things you already knew, or just plain anything that popped out at you.	1. 2. 3.

PICK A QUESTION

Use this space to review the study questions at the end of the chapter and respond to the one you find most thought-provoking or convicting.

EMPOWERING WORDS

- *Traditionalist Christian view*—Scripture teaches that sexual activity was designed for and intended to be enjoyed between a married man and woman.

- *Revisionist Christian view*—Since loving, consensual, monogamous, same-sex relations are not explicitly prohibited in Scripture, they can be blessed by God—even holy—and should be included in the life of the church.

- *Taboo*—Taboos are cultural prohibitions on behaviors which are deemed unnatural, unhealthy, or otherwise unacceptable.

- *Desensitization*—This is the process of exposing a person to a stimulus (an idea, a picture, etc.) so many times that it is seen as normal and no longer provokes an emotional response.

 ## ILLUSTRATING DESENSITIZATION

Ask your children if they have ever tried to approach an animal—a dog, a cat, or a bird—and had it run away from them. What about approaching a pet that knew them? From the perspective of the animal, why does one flee and the other respond happily? Talk with your children about how *familiarity breeds feelings of safety* and discuss how this also applies to our instinctual reactions to unbiblical worldviews. Sex-positivity relies on the process of desensitization.

EMPOWERING THOUGHTS

1. Culture tells our teens that social media presence leads to validation, and sexual promiscuity is a positive way to get to know yourself. According to the Christian worldview, how do we...

   a. Achieve validation? See Psalm 34:15.

   b. Get to know ourselves in a positive way? See Romans 12:3.

2. In 1 Corinthians 6:12, the apostle Paul explains, "'All things are lawful for me,' but not all things are helpful. 'All things are lawful for me,' but I will not be dominated by anything." How is the Christian view—that not every sexual act is beneficial— at odds with sex-positivity's claim that any consensual and pleasurable act is good?

3. What is the source of morality according to Scripture? Is it an objective or subjective source? Explain. (Hint: See pages 40-45 in chapter 2.)

4. Scripture talks about two different types of judgment—one of which is biblically condemned (Matthew 7:1-5; Luke 6:37-42; Romans 2:1-3) and one of which is biblically commanded (Leviticus 19:15; John 7:24; 1 Corinthians 5:11-13). What are the differences between these two types of judgment?

DIGGING DEEPER

1. Chapter 8 opens with a brief look at the origins of the sexual revolution of the '60s, especially the influence of Wilhelm Reich. To answer the questions below, see pages 131-132.

a. What was his goal?

b. What did he encourage?

c. What did he champion?

d. What did he assert led to health and even salvation?

2. As God's image-bearers, we are created with a divinely designed purpose that includes a compulsion to worship. Of course, we are to worship God who alone does all things motivated out of pure love, goodness, and understanding of what leads to human flourishing.

Reich's materialistic view of the universe does not allow for the existence of a supernatural God, but even he demonstrates this God-given compulsion to worship.

a. What do your answers above reveal about the object of Reich's worship?

b. What do you think it means to worship?

c. Where have you been tempted to direct your worship?

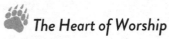 **The Heart of Worship**

Discuss with your children how they would define worship. It might include how a person spends their time or money, what they defend, what they talk about, what they include as their primary descriptors of themselves, etc. (It's usually a combination of all of these!) With older children, ask if they think our culture worships sex. What should our lives look like if we were to truly worship God? What is an area in your and your kids' lives that might qualify as worship? How are they purposefully integrating a worship of God into that area? What is the difference between worshipping one's hobbies and interests versus worshipping God *through* one's hobbies and interests?

It's Time to ROAR Like a Mother at Sex-Positivity

Recognize the Message

3. In your own words, what is sex-positivity?

4. Consider the three key points of sex-positivity. Which have you encountered most often and where? See pages 133-134.

5. Sometimes cultural taboos are evidence of God's law written on our hearts. How might you discern the difference between your own preferences and evidence of God's design?

6. How do you think a sex-positive person would evaluate a sexual act that was physically harmful, but to which a person had consented and claimed to enjoy? In what ways can sex-positivity be at odds with promoting health and wellbeing?

Offer Discernment

7. Identify and explain what we can learn from sex-positivity. What truths does it offer, or what motives can we dignify? See pages 134-135.

8. Identify and explain the seven main lies of sex-positivity (pages 135-140). Highlight or underline the three that, in your opinion, most greatly undermine the biblical sexual ethic. Share with your group which three lies you selected and discuss why. For each lie, provide an example of a biblical truth that is twisted by sex-positivity.

LIE	EXPLANATION	WHAT BIBLICAL TRUTH IS TWISTED BY THIS LIE?
If it's consensual, it's moral.		
Pleasure is the only purpose of sex.		
All judgments (except this one!) are wrong!		
Sex-positivity leads to freedom.		
All expressions of sexuality are healthy.		

LIE	EXPLANATION	WHAT BIBLICAL TRUTH IS TWISTED BY THIS LIE?
You can be a sex-positive Christian.		
If you're not for us, you're sex-negative!		

Argue for a Healthier Approach

9. Consider the three truths listed on pages 141-142. Which do you think is most challenging for kids to understand, and why?

Reinforce with Discussion, Discipleship, and Prayer

10. Give your own examples of how children can be taught to understand the consequences of having no rules.

11. How can we explain to our kids the difference between using good judgment and being judgmental?

KEY SCRIPTURES

We encourage you to read the following verses in context (meaning, read at least the entire chapter). Reflect on how they relate to what you're learning, and thank God for the hope and guidance found in His Word.

- Ephesians 4:30—"Do not grieve the Holy Spirit of God, by whom you were sealed for the day of redemption."

- Psalm 25:9—"He leads the humble in what is right, and teaches the humble his way."

- Galatians 5:1—"For freedom Christ has set us free; stand firm therefore, and do not submit again to a yoke of slavery."

- Romans 1:25—"They exchanged the truth about God for a lie and worshiped and served the creature rather than the Creator, who is blessed forever!"

PAWS FOR PRAYER

In closing this chapter, reflect on what you learned in lesson 8 and journal your prayer to God here:

Praise:

Admit:

Worship with thanksgiving:

Supplication (ask):

Part Three

THINGS THAT ARE TRIPPING EVERYONE UP

In part one, we learned what God wants to communicate through human sexuality. We learned about the power of sex and how destructive it is when misused. We also defined and explained the beauty of a biblical worldview, including how it affects the way we view sexuality. In part two, we learned about an unbiblical worldview that is shaping and influencing public education and secular thought today.

As we turn the last corner into part three, we will take a closer look at how these false teachings sneak into our lives, the lives of our kids, and even the lives of our churches—justifying their presence under the new "biblical" interpretations of love and inclusivity. We will look at each issue, identify where the church has fallen short and compromised, and set our sights on how we can love people better—the way the Bible says. The gospel is our greatest hope; we are all equal at the foot of the cross, equally fallen and equally offered redemption.

LESSON 9

PORNOGRAPHY

The younger a child is when they are exposed to suggestive images, the earlier their brains can be rewired to seek instant gratification and pleasure. They're also less likely to perceive the dangers and consequences of what they're viewing because the good judgment portion of the brain doesn't fully develop until adulthood. They just see a hot chick, so they'll buy the video game, or watch the movie with the shirtless hunk, and click on the website to see more because it feels good. The adult entertainment industry knows this and is happy to meet their demand. In short: they're using our kids' brains against them, grooming them to be *sensual* consumers instead of sensible ones. How do they get them to be sensual consumers? By hijacking the brain and using its chemicals against them.

Mama Bear Apologetics Guide to Sexuality, page 152

ACTIVE READING NOTES

READING FOCUS	MY RESPONSE
Before You Read:	
After skimming the chapter title and subheads, what is one question you would like to have answered in the chapter?	My question:
While You Read:	
Vocabulary List three words you found in the chapter in addition to the words we have provided.	My words: Book words: *oxytocin* (page 153)— *vasopressin* (page 153)— *dopamine* (page 154)—
After You Read:	
Answer Did you find an answer to your pre-reading question? (We hope so.) If yes, write it down.	My answer:

"Aha!" moments	My "Aha!" moments:
List three things you highlighted or underlined in the chapter. This can be new information you learned, encouraging reinforcements of things you already knew, or just plain anything that popped out at you.	1. 2. 3.

PICK A QUESTION

Use this space to review the study questions at the end of the chapter and respond to the one you find most thought-provoking or convicting.

EMPOWERING WORDS

- *Exploitation*—Exploitation is the act of taking advantage of someone for selfish gain.

- *Addiction*—Addiction occurs when a person engages in an action to the point where it is no longer a choice but a compulsion. In order to achieve feelings of euphoria, they must increasingly escalate the behavior. Due to physiological adaptation, the drive toward the behavior is often no longer motivated on feeling the "high" but rather on merely feeling *normal.*

- *(Sexual) grooming*—This is the creation of an interpersonal bond and sense of safety for the purpose of exploiting an individual. Grooming involves intentionally eroding personal boundaries through escalating levels of touch or sexualized content for the purpose of exploiting a person sexually. Often, grooming involves play-acting, discussing, or viewing sexualized material to where the intended victim begins to see these behaviors as normal. Once the grooming process is complete, the victimized individual will often *voluntarily* participate in sexual activities they would never have consented to before the grooming process.

- *Pornography*—Pornography is any sexually explicit material whose primary goal is to elicit sexual arousal in the viewers.

EMPOWERING THOUGHTS

"Fight the New Drug" (www.FightTheNewDrug.org) is a non-religious organization united around exposing the devastation caused by pornography to individuals, relationships, and societies. Their website hosts resources including scientific studies, testimonials, and even a documentary series uncovering many of the same troubling trends we discuss in this chapter. We recommend familiarizing yourself with this organization and the work they are doing.

1. How can an organization like this help us demonstrate the validity of the Bible's teachings on human sexuality to our children?

2. How can this organization and its research open up conversations with friends and family who don't come from a Christian background?

3. How would you define *obscenity* and *pornography*?

DIGGING DEEPER

1. On pages 150-152, we learn some troubling facts about the scope of the pornography problem. Which of the statistics horrified you the most, and why?

2. What makes porn potentially more addictive than other drugs? See pages 154-155.

3. "When it comes to pornography, it is not the amount of pornography, but the *type* that changes" (page 155). Explain the significance of this statement.

4. What are the two most commonly used descriptors of pornography? See page 157.

a. Summarize what is meant by *objectification*. See pages 157-158.

b. Summarize what is meant by *dehumanization*. See pages 158-159.

 An Exit Strategy for Porn Exposure

Our kids need a way to recuse themselves when their friends are looking at porn. If you want to talk with your son about the dangers of pornography, it'll be key to get his dad or a trusted male mentor involved and to equip them with the statistics. Your son needs to practice the conversation that will get him out of a tough situation and be prepared with responses that won't leave him belittled or emasculated. He might say something like:

- "Have fun with your fake sex; I'm not quite that desperate."

- "You *do* realize a lot of the women you're watching were trafficked, right?"

- "Are you *trying* to win the record for Youngest Case of Erectile Dysfunction?"

Porn isn't just a boy problem. Anyone can become addicted to it due to the chemicals involved. Our girls need a way to say no too. This is where we need to emphasize the reality of sex trafficking and how it doesn't start in a seedy hotel room. It begins with seeing sexualized images and then wanting to imitate them in order to be popular and accepted. Your job as a parent—especially for dads—is to give your girls the attention, healthy touch, and affirmation they so desperately crave.

As your girls get older, they will be tempted to post pictures of themselves on their social media that imitate their favorite celebrities. Ask your girls to pay attention to their images: Is their *face and smile* the main attraction? The company in the photograph or the event they attended? Or is the picture primarily about their bodies, sexy faces, or what they are wearing? If the photo only serves the purpose of looking sexy—mainly showcasing their bodies or bedroom eyes—talk to them about what it means to objectify themselves and why this is not a route they want to take. And don't be shy about monitoring your teen's social media! If you see a concerning post, talk to them about what motivated them to take and post the picture. Remember: Guys lust, and girls lust to be lusted after.

If your kids are younger, it's never too early to talk about good pictures and bad pictures. Explain to your kids that the Internet is full of pictures of body parts that God made for us to keep private. Warn them that they'll very likely encounter those pictures online. If they do, they'll probably have one of two reactions: They'll either feel embarrassed and scared to tell anyone, or they'll feel curious and want to find more pictures like that. Remind your kids that *both* reactions are normal—and the correct response is always to immediately tell a parent, teacher, or other trusted adult what they've seen.

It's Time to ROAR Like a Mother at Pornography

Recognize the Message

1. In your own words, how would you define pornography?

2. "We have underestimated the enemy and wandered onto the battlefield totally unarmed." Write the sentence that immediately follows the one above on page 159.

3. Consider the three main messages of pornography on pages 159-160. What are the ramifications for a child who believes these lies are true? Can you think of any popular books or movies that promote one of these messages?

MAIN MESSAGE	RAMIFICATIONS	EXAMPLE FROM POP CULTURE

Offer Discernment

1. What are some legitimate needs people might seek to meet with pornography? What would be a legitimate way to meet those needs? See pages 161-162.

2. Consider the six main lies of porn on pages 162-165. Which three do you consider to be the most enslaving, and why?

   •

   •

   •

Is It Porn If the Characters Are Married?

As Christians, we've taught our kids that sex between a husband and a wife is beautiful. But one of the ways that porn is becoming mainstream is by smuggling in graphic scenes of sex between married adults. Ask your older kids if it's okay for us to watch graphic sex if the characters are married. Why or why not?

Furthermore, sex scenes on film and TV are choreographed and manipulated. This leads to confusion for newly married couples who struggle to reconcile sex in the real world with what they saw portrayed in the movies. (As my sister-in-law stated matter-of-factly to me pre-marriage: "It's not like the movies. Prepare for a lot more...um...noises.")

As you're skipping graphic scenes when your kids are watching movies with you, explain why! Exploring your sexuality with a spouse is a lot more fun when you don't have to first unlearn what media has told you.

Argue for a Healthier Approach

1. Fill in the blanks from page 166: "God created the act of sex for _____ and _____ to recommit to each other _____ and to connect with another in a way that transcends _____ or _____."

2. Complete these two sentences (page 166):

   a. Who (or what) you share your orgasm with matters, *and*

   _____

   _____.

   b. There will likely be some emotional (and physiological) consequences, *and* _____.

Reinforce with Discussion, Discipleship, and Prayer

Make a list of four healthy behaviors/experiences that your child (or you) really enjoy (the fun, dopamine-producing things):

-
-
-
-

Are these things part of your regular routine? If not, what steps can you take as a family to have more healthy fun together?

KEY SCRIPTURES

We encourage you to read the following verses in context (meaning, read at least the entire chapter). Reflect on how they relate to what you're learning, and thank God for the hope and guidance found in His Word.

- Luke 4:18—"The Spirit of the Lord is upon me, because he has anointed me to proclaim good news to the poor. He has sent me to proclaim liberty to the captives and recovering of sight to the blind, to set at liberty those who are oppressed."

- Proverbs 4:23—"Keep your heart with all vigilance, for from it flow the springs of life."

- Psalm 66:16—"Come and hear, all you who fear God, and I will tell what he has done for my soul."

- Matthew 6:22-23—"The eye is the lamp of the body. So, if your eye is healthy, your whole body will be full of light, but if your eye is bad, your whole body will be full of darkness. If then the light in you is darkness, how great is the darkness!"

PAWS FOR PRAYER

In closing this chapter, reflect on what you learned in lesson 9 and journal your prayer to God here:

Praise:

Admit:

Worship with thanksgiving:

Supplication (ask):

LESSON 10

SAME-SEX
ATTRACTION

We have to be the generation to disciple our children to truly love and understand their same-sex-attracted peers while maintaining a commitment to biblical truth about marriage. Because...if we mess with the picture God gave us through sex, marriage, and gender, we mess with people's ability to see God accurately. Who among us is willing to stand before God and say that they encouraged people to remain in bondage to a distorted view of Him when it was His desire for them to walk in freedom? We cannot afford to get this one wrong, Mama Bears.

Mama Bear Apologetics Guide to Sexuality, page 175

ACTIVE READING NOTES

READING FOCUS	MY RESPONSE
Before You Read:	
After skimming the chapter title and subheads, what is one question you would like to have answered in the chapter?	My question:
While You Read:	
Vocabulary List three words you found in the chapter in addition to the words we have provided.	My words: Book words: *false dichotomy* (page 175)— *attachment theory* (page 177)— *eisegesis* (page 182)—
After You Read:	
Answer Did you find an answer to your pre-reading question? (We hope so.) If yes, write it down.	My answer:

"Aha!" moments	My "Aha!" moments:
List three things you highlighted or underlined in the chapter. This can be new information you learned, encouraging reinforcements of things you already knew, or just plain anything that popped out at you.	1. 2. 3.

PICK A QUESTION

Use this space to review the study questions at the end of the chapter and respond to the one you find most thought-provoking or convicting.

EMPOWERING WORDS

- *Systematic theology*—This term describes the study of what the whole Bible teaches about any given topic or issue.

- *Doctrine of inerrancy*—This doctrine affirms that Scripture (in its original manuscripts) is without error, and we can trust it to accurately convey the words of God.

- *Exegesis*—Exegesis is the systematic study and teaching of Scripture in light of its original context and intended meaning.

- *Heteronormative*—The assumption that sexual attraction toward the opposite gender is (or should be) the norm. This word is used by trans activists and queer theorists to describe the harm and oppression caused by this assumption.

EMPOWERING THOUGHTS

Take some time to read the story of Jesus' encounter with the Samaritan woman in John 4:4-42. Keep in mind the Samaritans were a race of people the Jews utterly despised, and this woman was considered a scandalous, immoral social outcast even to her own people. She is at the well alone—intentionally coming at a time when no one else would be there. But it's in that place where she meets Jesus. This is a well-known story, but God's Word is so good at touching our hearts in new ways every time we go to it. As you read the story, consider the following questions:

1. How does Jesus lead with relationship (not legalism) in His encounter with this immoral woman?

2. The Samaritan woman has deep emotional needs, and she has sin in her life. Which does Jesus address first? What is her need?

3. How does the woman emotionally respond to Jesus?

4. Jesus doesn't compromise truth, but who is the one to bring the Samaritan woman's sin into the conversation first?

5. How does Jesus' encounter with her affirm the Samaritan woman's value?

6. How can this story inform the way we love and relate to same-sex attracted family and friends in our own lives?

 Review the Four Loves

Review the material on the four loves in lesson 7. Look for further opportunities this week to reinforce this concept with your kids, frequently asking them to identify which types of love they're seeing portrayed. This can even be brought into your family devotions and Bible reading. For example, in the story of the Samaritan woman at the well, what kind of love had she lived her life in service to? What kind of love did she experience during her encounter with Jesus?

Whose Law Are We Talking About?

Time for a civics lesson! On a large piece of paper, draw a Venn diagram with two overlapping circles. Label the circles *God's Law* and *Government's Law*. Together, name as many laws as you can think of and decide where each one should be placed. Where do God's law and civic laws overlap? Where do they differ? For instance, you might come up with "Do not murder," which would belong in the circles' shared space. Or perhaps your kids think of "When turning left in traffic, merge into the first available legal lane." Traffic laws would go in the government circle. This exercise can be helpful in explaining the legalization of same-sex marriage, showing your children that while same-sex marriage is legal, that doesn't make it approved by God.

DIGGING DEEPER

1. Fill in the blanks below from page 173:

   • Same-sex attraction is not the _____ sin.

   • The gospel is not about making _____ people
     _____.

   • The gospel is about _____ sinners
     into _____ of God.

2. If your child comes to you saying they are gay or transgender, it is important to respond with gentleness and compassion. What are the four things we should do listed in the second paragraph on page 174?

   • _____

   • _____

   • _____

     _____

• _____

_____

3. On page 175, it says that often people who embrace LGBTQ+ as part of God's design end up "leaving biblical inerrancy in the dustbin as they go." Have you ever seen this happen? What do you think happens to a person's theology and faith in the long run once they deny that Scripture is God's infallible Word to humans?

4. On pages 176-178, we describe the scientific and sociological difficulties with drawing conclusions about homosexuality. Why do you think there is such a push to explain homosexuality from a scientific perspective?

5. Thought experiment: What if—one day—a gene was discovered that caused homosexual desires in some people. Would that change what Christians believe according to the Bible? Why or why not?

What Do We Mean by "Dignity and Respect"?

Many parents are not quite sure what to do when a child's friend or family member comes out as gay. We want to explain what is happening, but we don't want our child running to them and reminding them that they are in sin—because we are *all* in sin, honey-child. How can we as parents guide this conversation? Remember the "image of God" game from page 50? This is super important to reinforce. But the question remains, "What does it mean in practicality to treat someone as an image-bearer with dignity and respect who is not currently *reflecting* the imago dei?" The main issue is to interact with them as individuals, without participating (even passively) in the sin. Brainstorm the difference with your children. Playing games at recess? Dignity and respect. Helping them ask out a same-sex crush? Participating. Make a list of activities which will promote dignity and respect without affirming unbiblical ideas.

It's Time to ROAR Like a Mother at Same-Sex Attraction

Recognize the Message

1. List and summarize the six main passages in Scripture that address homosexuality:

   a.

   b.

c.

d.

e.

f.

2. What are the two main camps when it comes to interpreting what the Bible teaches on homosexuality?

3. How is the alternative nomenclature of "affirming" and "non-affirming" a rhetorical tactic to paint the traditional Christian view as unloving?

4. List and summarize six common arguments given by revisionists for rejecting the traditionalist view (pages 179-181). Have you found yourself in agreement with any of these?

a.

b.

c.

d.

e.

f.

Offer Discernment

1. List and summarize the biblical responses to the revisionist arguments above. See pages 181-185.

   a.

   b.

   c.

   d.

   e.

   f.

Argue for a Healthier Approach

1. Fill in the blank from page 185: "We don't want the church to be divided over this issue anymore, but there is no _____ apart from the unity of _____."

2. List and summarize in 1-2 sentences the four important reminders on pages 185-187.

   a.

   b.

   c.

   d.

3. Which of the above truths challenges you the most?

Are You Prepared for a Situation Like This?

A concerned Mama Bear recently contacted me about a sticky situation. Her daughter's school was having a "Wear Orange for LGBT+ Day." What could her daughter do? If she wore orange, she was affirming a cause she did not affirm. But if she didn't wear orange, she would stand out from the whole school and be labeled a hater and a bully.

I wasn't sure what to say at first, so I sat on it for a few days. After much prayer, I suggested that it might be a *great* day to schedule her daughter's yearly physical. Unfortunately, my response was too late. Her daughter went ahead and wore orange rather than draw attention to herself, and I felt like I'd failed them for not responding sooner.

In hindsight, you can only have so many kids visiting the doctor at once; they will have to face the mob sooner or later. What response will be both loving toward unbelievers while still allowing our children to be set apart—as God has called all believers to be?

Discuss this situation with your kids. While the apostle Paul exhorts us, "If possible, so far as it depends on you, live peaceably with all" (Romans 12:18), sometimes our best efforts still won't be enough. The world will "heap abuse" on us for not joining in with them (1 Peter 4:4 NIV). Here is where we can remind our kids that hostility will come to us when we choose to follow Christ. Are we willing to endure the hostility for the sake of His name and a clear conscience? How can we as Christians prepare for this hostility without it becoming a self-fulfilling prophecy?

Reinforce with Discussion, Discipleship, and Prayer

1. Learning how to relate to people with truth *and* love is a huge part of living like Jesus. Brainstorm two or three situations in which we might need to tell a friend a hard truth (not about sexuality), and how we can do it with love. Also discuss how differently

things could go if the truth was delivered without love. (For example: "I think you spend too much time on your phone.")

2. In the chapter we learned that same-sex attraction might be a symptom, not a root cause. Listening well to someone's story can help us differentiate between symptoms and root causes. Describe a situation in your life when someone listened to you well and empowered you to discern an underlying truth.

KEY SCRIPTURES

We encourage you to read the following verses in context (meaning, read at least the entire chapter). Reflect on how they relate to what you're learning, and thank God for the hope and guidance found in His Word.

- Hebrews 4:15-16—"We do not have a high priest who is unable to sympathize with our weaknesses, but one who in every respect has been tempted as we are, yet without sin. Let us then with confidence draw near to the throne of grace, that we may receive mercy and find grace to help in time of need."

- 2 Peter 2:18—"Speaking loud boasts of folly, they entice by sensual passions of the flesh those who are barely escaping from those who live in error."

- 1 Corinthians 6:11—"You were washed, you were sanctified, you were justified in the name of the Lord Jesus Christ and by the Spirit of our God."

- 2 Timothy 2:15—"Do your best to present yourself to God as one approved, a worker who has no need to be ashamed, rightly handling the word of truth."

- 1 Thessalonians 4:8—"Whoever disregards this [instruction on sexuality], disregards not man but God, who gives his Holy Spirit to you."

PAWS FOR PRAYER

In closing this chapter, reflect on what you learned in lesson 10 and journal your prayer to God here:

Praise:

Admit:

Worship with thanksgiving:

Supplication (ask):

GENDER IDENTITY

The political push to separate biological sex from gender makes an already tumultuous time that much more chaotic. How in the world can we expect to help our kids to grow into men and women of God if they aren't even sure what it means to be a man or a woman? And what happened to make us question this aspect of our identity? It used to be a no-brainer. It was this *one beautiful thing* that we didn't have to "figure out." It never even occurred to most of us.

Mama Bear Apologetics Guide to Sexuality, page 192

ACTIVE READING NOTES

READING FOCUS	MY RESPONSE
Before You Read:	
After skimming the chapter title and subheads, what is one question you would like to have answered in the chapter?	My question:
While You Read:	
Vocabulary List three words you found in the chapter in addition to the words we have provided.	My words: Book words: *SRY gene* (page 197)— *intersex* (page 198)—
After You Read:	
Answer Did you find an answer to your pre-reading question? (We hope so.) If yes, write it down.	My answer:

"Aha!" moments	My "Aha!" moments:
List three things you highlighted or underlined in the chapter. This can be new information you learned, encouraging reinforcements of things you already knew, or just plain anything that popped out at you.	1. 2. 3.

PICK A QUESTION

Use this space to review the study questions at the end of the chapter and respond to the one you find most thought-provoking or convicting.

EMPOWERING WORDS

- *Gender queer*—A person who rejects biological gender distinctions and identifies with neither, both, or a combination of male and female genders often self-defines as gender queer.

- *Gender fluid*—This term describes someone whose gender identity fluctuates instead of remaining fixed.

- *Social transition*—When an individual changes their gender presentation, they go through this nonsurgical process. This might include changing one's pronouns, name, and style of dress.

- *Cisnormative*—The assumption that identifying as one's biological gender is (or should be) the norm. This word is used by trans activists and queer theorists to describe the oppression caused by binary gender language.

- *Gender confirmation surgery (GCS)*—GCS is the surgical component of transitioning. "Top surgery" refers to either removing or augmenting breast tissue, and "bottom surgery" refers to genital reconstruction to match the desired gender.

- *Gender-affirming therapy*—Gender dysphoria treatment focuses on prioritizing a person's self-perceived gender identity over their biological sex.

EMPOWERING THOUGHTS

Gender roles are the social norms that reflect a particular culture's interpretation of masculinity and femininity. These societal "rules" can be quite different depending upon where and when someone lives. Most of us can agree these arbitrary standards have led to oppressive stereotypes and faulty expectations for men and women throughout history. Fast-forward to Western culture today, and gender itself is being defined as the internal sense of self as female, male, both, or neither—basically what someone feels they are based upon these stereotypes. Remember the discussion of *identity* on pages 116-119? Why might basing one's gender on shifting cultural stereotypes lead to confusion rather than clarity?

Two hot trends you might not be aware of are Christian kids identifying as bisexual and/or nonbinary. These two identities allow them to be a part of the LGBTQ+ community while technically retaining their cisgender heterosexual practices. First, you need to be aware that this is happening in your community. Second, equip yourself to respond to it—and prepare your kids for the peer-pressure to participate. A kid who is prepared for peer pressure is less likely to fall for it.

DIGGING DEEPER

1. Consider the deep meaning that comes from the root word *gen*—the Latin and Greek roots for "that which produces" or "birth"—and the significance it gives the word *gender*. Now compare it to how the word *gender* is defined in modern culture. How is this an example of linguistic theft? How is it making people talk past one another?

2. Fill in the blanks with words from the word bank (pages 194-197).

gender	gender dysphoria	cisgender	transgender female
transgender male		binary	intersex

a. _____ is anything that has only two options.

b. _____ is the sex by which a person psychologically self-identifies.

c. _____ refers to a person who feels uncomfortable or mismatched with their biological sex.

d. _____ a biological male who self-identifies as a female (MtF).

   e._____ is when a person is born with a
   genetic, hormonal, and sometimes genital variation from the
   traditional understanding of chromosomal sex.

   f. _____ is a biological female who self-
   identifies as a male (FtM).

3. What is the short answer for what science shows about gender?
   See page 197.

4. Summarize what you learned about the role of testosterone
   from pages 198-199 and what we want our kids to understand
   about its role.

5. In one sentence, what does the Bible say about transgenderism
   and gender expression? See Deuteronomy 22:5.

 ## Gender Expression in the Bible

The Bible shows that men and women have great freedom when
it comes to gender expression. Ask your kids how the following biblical figures defy modern Western gender stereotypes.

a. David (1 Samuel 16:23)

b. Deborah (Judges 4:4)

c. Jacob (Genesis 25:27-29)

d. The Virtuous Wife (Proverbs 31:10-31)

e. Any others you can think of

It's Time to ROAR Like a Mother at Gender Identity

Recognize the Message

1. How would you define *gender identity* in your own words?

2. How would you define *gender roles* in your own words?

3. Consider the six main messages of gender theory and trans-genderism on pages 200-201. Which, if believed, would most undermine the traditional understanding of gender and why?

4. The entire scientific method is based on measurable observations. How would inserting private, subjective experience undermine the scientific method?

 Perception or Reality?

Remember the discussion on desensitization in lesson 8? One thing that's being repeated to our kids from kindergarten to college—not to mention in the media—is that gender identity and biological sex can be different. This has been repeated so many times that our children accept it as true—just because it's so familiar. This is equating perception with reality. Discuss with your children how our feelings don't always line up with reality—no matter how strongly they are felt. *This* is the message we need to be repeating to our kids ad nauseum. See maxim #7 on page 249 for help.

Offer Discernment

5. List two personal takeaways from the discussion of what the church can learn from the transgender community on pages 201-203.

6. Consider and briefly explain the four lies of gender identity on pages 203-205. Which lie have you encountered most

frequently? How might you teach your children to respond to this lie?

-
-
-
-

Argue for a Healthier Approach

7. There is so much confusion in our world regarding what it means to be a man or a woman. Which of the four ways the Bible addresses this (pages 205-207) do you believe is hardest for today's youth to accept or understand? Why?

Reinforce with Discussion, Discipleship, and Prayer

1. Romans 2:4 informs us that God's kindness draws people to repentance. As God's image-bearers, our kindness can play a huge role in helping lost or broken people find His unconditional love. Brainstorm ways you and your children can, without compromising truth, reflect God's kindness more intentionally to those around you.

2. Often, when engaging in hot-button issues, we forget that hearts are involved. Set aside time to ask your children to imagine how others might feel in different situations (not just painful ones). Model compassion and empathy with

your children even in times when you must stand firm on consequences for disobedience.

3. One of a believer's biggest temptations is to prioritize being understood over understanding another person. How might seeking to understand people *first* build a bridge to mutual understanding?

4. Read 2 Samuel 12 with your children. Nathan chose to deliver a difficult message to David by first appealing to an area of agreement. How can we use this same principle to understand and be understood by those around us when it comes to dicey topics?

KEY SCRIPTURES

We encourage you to read the following verses (meaning, read at least the entire chapter). Reflect on how they relate to what you're learning, and thank God for the hope and guidance found in His Word.

- Psalm 139:13—"You formed my inward parts; you knitted me together in my mother's womb."

- Job 33:4—"The Spirit of God has made me, and the breath of the Almighty gives me life."

- Micah 6:8—"He has told you, O man, what is good; and what does the LORD require of you but to do justice, and to love kindness, and to walk humbly with your God?"

- Romans 6:6-7—"Our old self was crucified with him in order that the body of sin might be brought to nothing, so that we would no longer be enslaved to sin. For one who has died has been set free from sin."

PAWS FOR PRAYER

In closing this chapter, reflect on what you learned in lesson 11 and journal your prayer to God here:

Praise:

Admit:

Worship with thanksgiving:

Supplication (ask):

LESSON 12

PURITY
CULTURE

Kids, too, often felt pressured by pushy parents or friends to make a pledge they weren't ready for or didn't fully understand. They knew they didn't want to let their youth pastor or mom down, so they played the part...until the boyfriend or girlfriend came along, that is....Overly zealous church leaders made virginity their primary focus, neglecting the redemptive work of Christ. Some even ignored the original design of the curriculum by excluding parents, refusing to be transparent about what was being taught, or by integrating their own perverted twists to the lessons.

Mama Bear Apologetics Guide to Sexuality, page 217

ACTIVE READING NOTES

READING FOCUS	MY RESPONSE
Before You Read:	
After skimming the chapter title and subheads, what is one question you would like to have answered in the chapter?	My question:
While You Read:	
Vocabulary List three words you found in the chapter in addition to the words we have provided.	My words: Book words: *chastity* (page 221) — *sexual integrity* (page 226) —
After You Read:	
Answer Did you find an answer to your pre-reading question? (We hope so.) If yes, write it down.	My answer:

"Aha!" moments	My "Aha!" moments:
List three things you highlighted or underlined in the chapter. This can be new information you learned, encouraging reinforcements of things you already knew, or just plain anything that popped out at you.	1. 2. 3.

PICK A QUESTION

Use this space to review the study questions at the end of the chapter and respond to the one you find most thought-provoking or convicting.

EMPOWERING WORDS

- *Covenant*—A covenant is an agreement between two parties that establishes their relational identity to one another as well as their roles within the relationship.

- *Inherited guilt*—This doctrine says we are all counted guilty because God has righteously imputed Adam's guilt to all of us (Romans 5:12-21).

- *Inherited corruption*—This doctrine teaches we are all born having inherited a sinful nature through Adam (Psalm 51:1-5).

- *Regeneration*—A supernatural act of God, regeneration makes us new as He imparts new spiritual life to us (John 3:3-8).

EMPOWERING THOUGHTS

Many people read the original sexual purity curriculum and find very little if anything they disagree with. In its infancy, purity curricula set out to engage both youth groups and parents in the meaningful role of lovingly and intentionally discipling children in biblical sexuality. Over time, the messaging became distorted—even abusive. Rather than holiness and freedom, the fruit was often shame and fear.

1. Why do good teachings often get distorted beyond recognition?

2. How did purity culture eventually distort or even contradict the doctrine of salvation by grace through faith?

3. Did your church or school teach using any of the purity culture curricula? Was your experience positive or negative? How did the teaching either (1) help you understand the truth of the gospel more clearly or (2) distort the gospel message?

4. Our sexuality and sexual ethic develop over time and are influenced by multiple players: parents, church, school, culture (especially social media), life experience, and peers.

 a. Which of these influences played the most significant role in the development of your own sexuality and sexual ethic?

 b. If you could talk to your teenage self, which misconception would you like to correct?

 c. How might you encourage parents who minimize their role or who believe they are too late to influence their children's beliefs about sexuality?

 Purity Versus Protection

Purity culture tends to emphasize (duh) purity. But remember the discussion from lessons 1, 2, and 3. Sexual faithfulness isn't just about "purity." It is about understanding *the God who is* while safeguarding ourselves from a force that is so powerful it requires protection and boundaries.

Ask your kids what they do to protect themselves from the sun. They might mention sunglasses, sunscreen, hats, etc. Remind them that God's commands regarding sexuality are put in place for their protection. How is protecting oneself a purer motive than guarding our reputations?

DIGGING DEEPER

1. Complete the following paragraph by filling in the blanks from page 214:

   Our kids deserve the truth—that God's plan for sex starts with marriage—but when the truth has been abused and twisted by the people we trust most, it no longer looks attractive...and can seem downright terrifying. We don't abandon _____ because of its _____. We _____ the abuses and stand firm in the _____.

2. Which biblical truths did the original purity curricula emphasize?

3. What were some unintended consequences of the purity message gone wrong?

4. Have you experienced any of the unintended baggage brought about by purity culture in your own life? If so, share briefly.

5. What are some ways in which the missteps or lies of purity culture might have affected girls differently than boys?

It's Time to ROAR Like a Mother at Purity Culture

Recognize the Message

1. In your own words, explain what is damaging about each of the three purity culture missteps discussed on pages 218-221.

2. Finally, correct the distortion with a statement that is theologically true and directly refutes the message and the damage.

THE MESSAGE	THE DAMAGE	HEALTHY TRUTH STATEMENT

3. Purity culture told girls their bodies could be stumbling blocks over which boys might trip. Stumbling blocks are objects. Though opposite to the desired goal, can you think of ways in which pornography and purity culture might lead to similar ends?

Offer Discernment

1. What important distinction related to holiness and chastity was missing from much of the purity movement? See page 221.

2. Many students mistakenly thought their physical virginity was essential for _____. See page 221.

3. How do our clothing choices actually communicate something about us?

4. Consider the three lies of purity culture. Which could bring the most baggage into a good marriage?

Argue for a Healthier Approach

1. Redemption is possible for _____. No amount of sexual brokenness can keep you from the _____ power of God (page 224).

2. Define *chastity* and share in your own words what we want our kids to understand about it (pages 224-226). ˙

3. What is the best guiding principle for choosing the clothes we will wear? See pages 225-226.

Reinforce with Discussion, Discipleship, and Prayer

We want our children to understand that clothes can send a message but avoid the temptation (and sometimes danger) of drawing wrong conclusions or forming harsh or hurtful judgments. We want to cultivate discernment clothed with kindness and mercy—thinking the best of others (Philippians 4:8). When reading books or watching television together, discuss what the face-value message of different outfits might be. Then discuss how those messages might differ from the true situation of the person in question.

KEY SCRIPTURES

We encourage you to read the following verses in context (meaning, read at least the entire chapter). Reflect on how they relate to what you're learning, and thank God for the hope and guidance found in His Word.

- Psalm 98:1—"Oh sing to the LORD a new song, for he has done marvelous things! His right hand and his holy arm have worked salvation for him."

- Isaiah 1:18—"Come now, let us reason together, says the LORD: though your sins are like scarlet, they shall be as white as snow; though they are red like crimson, they shall become like wool."

- Isaiah 61:10—"I will greatly rejoice in the LORD; my soul shall exult in my God, for he has clothed me with the garments of salvation; he has covered me with the robe of righteousness, as a bridegroom decks himself like a priest with a beautiful headdress, and as a bride adorns herself with her jewels."

- 1 Corinthians 10:31—"So, whether you eat or drink, or whatever you do, do all to the glory of God."

- Matthew 5:8—"Blessed are the pure in heart, for they shall see God."

PAWS FOR PRAYER

In closing this chapter, reflect on what you learned in lesson 12 and journal your prayer to God here:

Praise:

Admit:

Worship with thanksgiving:

Supplication (ask):

LESSON 13

TAKING UP YOUR SEXUAL CROSS

The call to discipleship with Jesus is a heavy one, and we shouldn't pretend otherwise with our kids. In Luke 9:23-24, Jesus says to His disciples, "Whoever wants to be my disciple must deny themselves and take up their cross daily and follow me. For whoever wants to save their life will lose it, but whoever loses their life for me will save it." Here, Jesus is saying bluntly that the Christian walk will not be an easy one; we'll all have burdens to bear. Is this scary? Yup. Do we know what crosses we'll be called to carry in our own individual lives? Nope. Do we know what crosses our *children* will be called to carry? Also, no. So what can we know?...[S]exual holiness is itself a cross we will have to carry—each one of us.

Mama Bear Apologetics Guide to Sexuality, pages 233-234

ACTIVE READING NOTES

READING FOCUS	MY RESPONSE
Before You Read:	
After skimming the chapter title and subheads, what is one question you would like to have answered in the chapter?	My question:
While You Read:	
Vocabulary List three words you found in the chapter in addition to the words we have provided.	My words: Book words: *encouragement* (page 232)— *imminent* (page 240)—
After You Read:	
Answer Did you find an answer to your pre-reading question? (We hope so.) If yes, write it down.	My answer:

"Aha!" moments	My "Aha!" moments:
List three things you highlighted or underlined in the chapter. This can be new information you learned, encouraging reinforcements of things you already knew, or just plain anything that popped out at you.	1. 2. 3.

PICK A QUESTION

Use this space to review the study questions at the end of the chapter and respond to the one you find most thought-provoking or convicting.

EMPOWERING WORDS

- *Sacrifice*—The act of offering to God something deeply precious at personal cost is a sacrifice.

- *Contempt*—When we feel that someone or something is beneath consideration, worthless, or deserving scorn, we have contempt.

- *Humility*—Humility is an accurate view of oneself grounded in who you are in Christ, so secure in God's love for you that you are willing to serve and sacrifice. Humility means not thinking too much or too little, too highly or too lowly, of oneself or others.

EMPOWERING THOUGHTS

Christians are called to take up their crosses. Some people see crosses as simply hardships—"thorns in the flesh" they are called to endure in life. This is only partly true. A real "cross to bear" involves something more than just trial and tribulation; a cross involves obedience and faithfulness *despite* this hardship. That is what distinguishes trials from crosses.

There are many false gospels out there promising your best life now through health, wealth, and prosperity. (We wrote about several of those in the first *Mama Bear Apologetics* book.) There are many false Jesuses out there who look more like personal assistants or authenticity coaches than the Lord of lords and King of kings. None of these prepares us for real life as a Christ-follower. None of these offers eternal hope, healing, and freedom from the pain of this world.

1. What are some of the empty, powerless, false messages you have heard recently from culture or even the church?

2. Do these reflect reality? Explain how these messages discourage rather than encourage people (page 232).

3. Read 2 Corinthians 2:23-33. List a few of the things Paul describes happening in his life.

4. Give one example of a popular encouragement that would fall utterly flat on Paul's ears.

How might a proper understanding of *encouragement* affect what you choose to read or listen to? What you post online? What do you think of apologists who seek to lovingly warn the church of deception?

DIGGING DEEPER

1. On page 232, we learn that we don't get to decide the right thing based on what's fair. How did Jesus model this in His earthly ministry?

2. Consider and summarize the ten crosses explained in the chapter (pages 234-239).

3. Do you or someone you love carry one of these crosses? How has it affected you or your loved one?

4. Do you feel a call or burden to individuals carrying one of these particular crosses? If so, which one?

5. Choose one or two crosses and share some ideas on how the church might more effectively help carry them.

 ### How Well Do We Know Our Neighbor's Cross?

Jesus calls us to take up our cross and follow Him. We take up our cross when we live with trials and tribulations and remain joyfully faithful to God. Consider a faithful member of your church community—someone well-known to your family. With this person's permission, or perhaps with their help (depending on your relationship), share with your children some of the crosses this person bears. Perhaps that carefree choir member is also patiently and lovingly caring for a special needs child. Perhaps the woman who is joyfully serving also struggles with chronic health conditions.

Help your children understand that *all* Christians carry crosses; the Christian life is not one of ease from burdens and trials. Establish in their minds that our Lord does not always lift us *out* of troubles; sometimes He hunkers down with us *in* them. Christians carry impossible burdens by the power of Christ Himself.

 Carrying Each Other's Burdens

Encourage your children to ask their friends what struggles they undergo, and ask them how those struggles affect their friends' lives. Teach your children to familiarize themselves with the struggles of others—and teach them to ask, "How can I help you carry this burden? How can I support you in this situation?"

One way to teach this to your kids? Model it! When your child comes home from school upset about friction in a relationship, ask her how you can help carry her burden.

KEY SCRIPTURES

We encourage you to read the following verses in context (meaning, read at least the entire chapter). Reflect on how they relate to what you're learning, and thank God for the hope and guidance found in His Word.

- 2 Corinthians 1:3-4—"Blessed be the God and Father of our Lord Jesus Christ, the Father of mercies and God of all comfort, who comforts us in all our affliction, so that we may be able to comfort those who are in any affliction, with the comfort with which we ourselves are comforted by God."

- Psalm 55:22—"Cast your burden on the Lord, and he will sustain you; he will never permit the righteous to be moved."

- Matthew 11:29—"Take my yoke upon you, and learn from me, for I am gentle and lowly in heart, and you will find rest for your souls."

- Romans 12:10—"Love one another with brotherly affection. Outdo one another in showing honor."

- 1 John 4:12—"No one has ever seen God; if we love one another, God abides in us and his love is perfected in us."

PAWS FOR PRAYER

In closing this chapter, reflect on what you learned in lesson 13 and journal your prayer to God here:

Praise:

Admit:

Worship with thanksgiving:

Supplication (ask):

ABOUT
THE AUTHORS

Hillary Morgan Ferrer, founder of Mama Bear Apologetics®, has a burden for providing accessible apologetics resources for busy moms. She has a master's in biology and her specialties are scientific apologetics, dealing with doubt, and identifying causes and solutions for youth leaving the church

Teasi Cannon is a wife, mother, teacher, author, and contributor to the Mama Bear Apologetics® ministry. Her passion for discipleship led her to obtain a master's degree in pastoral counseling from Liberty Theological Seminary. Teasi lives in Tennessee with her husband, Bill. They have three amazing grown children and one beloved son-in-law.

MAMA BEAR
APOLOGETICS

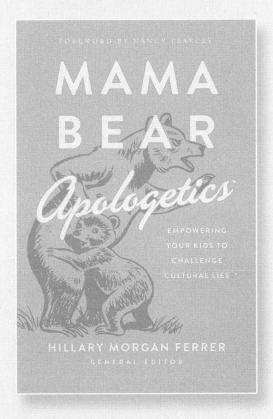

From a group of everyday Christian moms comes *Mama Bear Apologetics*®. This book equips you to teach your kids how to form their beliefs about what is true and what is false. Join bestselling author Hillary Morgan Ferrer in the Mama Bear movement—when you mess with our kids, we will demolish your arguments!

To learn more about Harvest House books and
to read sample chapters, visit our website:

www.HarvestHousePublishers.com

HARVEST HOUSE PUBLISHERS
EUGENE, OREGON